THE GEN Z PSYCHOLOGY

Unlocking the Secrets of a Digital Generation

Dr. Maxwell Shimba

Shimba Publishing, LLC
Printed in the United States of America

First Printing Edition 2024

TABLE OF CONTENTS

INTRODUCTION

Defining Generation Z

Generation Z, often abbreviated as Gen Z, refers to the cohort of individuals born roughly between the mid-1990s and the early 2010s. This generation follows the Millennials and is characterized by its distinct upbringing in an era of rapid technological advancement and significant societal changes. The exact dates defining Gen Z may vary among researchers, but the common consensus identifies those born from 1997 to 2012 as part of this generation. As the first true digital natives, Gen Z has grown up with the internet and mobile technology, shaping their identity, behaviors, and social interactions.

Demographics of Gen Z

Globally, Gen Z comprises a diverse and multicultural group. According to a report by the United Nations, there are over 2 billion individuals in this age group worldwide, representing approximately 32% of the global population.

This demographic diversity is marked by variations in ethnicity, culture, and socio-economic backgrounds, influencing their perspectives and experiences.

In the United States, Gen Z is the most racially and ethnically diverse generation to date. According to the Pew Research Center, nearly half of Gen Z identifies as non-white, with significant representation from Hispanic, Black, Asian, and multiracial backgrounds. This diversity fosters a sense of inclusivity and awareness of social issues, contributing to their values and beliefs, particularly regarding social justice, equity, and representation.

Economic Impact

As Gen Z transitions into adulthood, they are making their mark on the economy. With an estimated purchasing power of over $140 billion in the United States alone, their preferences and behaviors significantly influence market trends and brand strategies. This generation prioritizes authenticity, sustainability, and social responsibility in their purchasing decisions, compelling brands to adapt their marketing strategies to resonate with Gen Z values.

Psychological Profile

Understanding Gen Z's psychology requires an exploration of their unique cognitive and emotional development. Growing up in a fast-paced digital environment has influenced their attention spans, learning styles, and social interactions. Gen Z is adept at processing information quickly, often navigating multiple platforms simultaneously. This skill set reflects their ability to synthesize diverse sources of information, although it may also contribute to challenges in deep focus and mental health.

Furthermore, the pervasive presence of social media has reshaped Gen Z's social interactions and relationships. While they cultivate connections online, this generation grapples with the complexities of maintaining authentic relationships in an increasingly digital world. The impact of social media on their mental health, self-esteem, and interpersonal dynamics is a critical area of exploration, highlighting both the benefits and challenges of their digital lives.

Importance of Understanding Gen Z

As the world rapidly evolves, understanding Generation Z's unique characteristics and behaviors becomes increasingly essential for parents, educators, marketers, and employers. This generation will shape the future landscape across various sectors, from education and employment to social activism and consumerism. By gaining insights into their motivations, preferences, and values, stakeholders can better engage and support Gen Z in their personal and professional endeavors.

This chapter sets the foundation for a deeper exploration of Generation Z, delving into their digital landscape, psychological profiles, social interactions, buying decisions, and the broader cultural context that shapes their experiences. Through a comprehensive analysis of Gen Z, we can unlock valuable insights into the mindset of the most online generation yet, preparing for the challenges and opportunities they present in the coming years.

The Psychology of Gen Z

Understanding the psychology of Generation Z is essential for comprehending their behaviors, preferences, and the unique challenges they face. As digital natives, their psychological profile is shaped by the interplay of technology, social media, and significant global events that have marked their formative years. Here are key aspects of Gen Z psychology that complement the introductory overview:

1. Digital Natives and Cognitive Processing

Growing up with the internet, smartphones, and social media has led to a distinct cognitive style among Gen Z. They are accustomed to receiving information in rapid bursts, often consuming content through videos, memes, and short-form posts. This exposure to fast-paced media influences their attention spans, leading to an ability to multitask effectively, but it can also result in challenges related to deep focus and critical thinking.

Gen Z tends to exhibit strong analytical skills when processing information, often cross-referencing multiple sources before forming opinions. This behavior is driven by their awareness of misinformation and their desire for authenticity and accuracy. However, the sheer volume of information available can lead to information overload, contributing to anxiety and decision fatigue.

2. Emotional Intelligence and Social Connectivity

Despite being frequently labeled as "socially awkward" or overly reliant on technology, Gen Z is highly emotionally intelligent. They value empathy and inclusivity, seeking to connect with others on a deeper level. This generation is often more open about mental health issues, advocating for discussions around emotional well-being and seeking support through online platforms and communities.

Their social interactions, primarily facilitated through digital channels, allow for diverse connections but can also lead to feelings of isolation and loneliness. The pressure to maintain a curated online persona may heighten self-esteem issues, particularly when comparing themselves to others. As a result, mental health awareness is a significant focus for Gen Z, influencing how they navigate relationships and seek out resources for self-care.

3. Values-Driven Identity

Gen Z is a generation defined by its strong values, particularly concerning social justice, equality, and environmental sustainability. Their beliefs are often shaped by global events, such as climate change activism, racial justice movements, and political polarization. This generation is more likely to engage in activism, supporting brands and organizations that align with their values and taking a stand on issues they care about.

Their commitment to inclusivity and diversity is reflected in their friendships, workplace expectations, and consumption habits. Gen Z actively seeks representation and authenticity in media, demanding that brands reflect the diverse world in which they live. This desire for representation extends to their personal identities, as they embrace fluidity in gender, sexuality, and cultural expressions.

4. Adaptability and Resilience

The challenges faced by Gen Z—ranging from economic uncertainties to the impact of a global pandemic—have fostered a sense of adaptability and resilience. They have learned to navigate disruptions in education and employment with creativity and resourcefulness. This generation is often characterized by its entrepreneurial spirit, seeking unconventional paths and embracing gig work and online platforms to achieve their goals.

Their experiences have cultivated a pragmatic outlook, with many prioritizing financial stability and job security. However, this focus on practicality is balanced by a desire for meaningful work and a positive impact on society, driving them to seek out careers that align with their values.

5. Mental Health and Well-Being

Mental health is a critical aspect of Gen Z's psychological landscape. The pressure to excel academically, socially, and professionally, compounded by the constant connectivity of the digital world, can lead to increased anxiety and stress. As a result, this generation places a high value on mental health resources and self-care practices, advocating for destigmatization and accessibility to support services.

The pervasive influence of social media can have both positive and negative effects on their mental well-being. While online communities provide a sense of belonging and support, they can also contribute to feelings of inadequacy and comparison. Gen Z's willingness to engage in discussions about mental health reflects their proactive approach to seeking help and fostering a culture of openness around psychological struggles.

The psychology of Generation Z is characterized by a unique blend of adaptability, emotional intelligence, and a strong commitment to social values. Understanding these psychological underpinnings is essential for engaging with this generation, whether in educational settings, marketing strategies, or workplace environments. As we navigate the complexities of their digital and social worlds, recognizing their experiences and aspirations will be crucial in supporting their growth and development in an ever-changing landscape.

CHAPTER 1

GEN Z

Definition and Demographics

Generation Z, commonly referred to as Gen Z, encompasses individuals born approximately between 1997 and 2012. This generational cohort follows Millennials and precedes Generation Alpha. The exact dates defining the boundaries of Gen Z can vary slightly among researchers, but the overarching characteristics and experiences of this generation remain consistent across these boundaries.

Definition of Gen Z

Gen Z is the first generation to grow up with the internet and digital technology as integral parts of their daily lives from a young age. Unlike previous generations, they have never known a world without smartphones, social media, and instant access to information. This constant connectivity has profoundly shaped their worldview, communication styles, and social interactions.

Key characteristics defining Gen Z include:

1. Digital Natives: Born into a world where digital technology is ubiquitous, Gen Z is highly adept at using smartphones, tablets, and computers. They are proficient in navigating various digital platforms and are often early adopters of new technologies.

2. Global Connectivity: With the internet breaking down geographical barriers, Gen Z has a more global perspective than previous generations. They are exposed to diverse cultures and ideas through social media, streaming services, and online communities.

3. Value-Driven: Gen Z places a high value on social justice, inclusivity, and environmental sustainability. They are vocal about their beliefs and often use social media as a platform for advocacy and activism.

4. Instant Gratification: Accustomed to the immediacy of digital communication and instant access to information, Gen Z tends to expect quick responses and results. This trait influences their consumer behavior and interactions with brands.

5. Entrepreneurial Spirit: Many Gen Z individuals show a strong entrepreneurial inclination. They leverage digital tools to start businesses, create content, and monetize their skills and hobbies.

Demographics of Gen Z

Understanding the demographics of Gen Z is essential for comprehending their influence and impact on society. This section explores various demographic factors, including population size, geographic distribution, racial and ethnic diversity, education, and economic status.

1. Population Size:

- Gen Z constitutes a significant portion of the global population. In the United States alone, Gen Z represents approximately 20% of the total population, making them a critical demographic for marketers, educators, and policymakers.

2. Geographic Distribution:

- Gen Z is spread across urban, suburban, and rural areas, but there is a noticeable trend towards urbanization. Many Gen Z individuals are concentrated in major cities and metropolitan areas, attracted by opportunities for education, employment, and social activities.

3. Racial and Ethnic Diversity:

- Gen Z is the most racially and ethnically diverse generation in history. In the United States, nearly half of Gen

Z identifies as a racial or ethnic minority. This diversity is reflected in their cultural experiences, preferences, and values.

4. Education:

- Education is highly valued by Gen Z, with many pursuing higher education and specialized skills training. The generation has a higher rate of high school graduation compared to previous generations, and a significant proportion attends college or vocational training programs.

- Online learning and digital resources play a crucial role in their education, offering flexibility and access to a wide range of information.

5. Economic Status:

- Gen Z is entering the workforce during a time of economic uncertainty, influenced by factors such as the COVID-19 pandemic and rapid technological advancements. Many are concerned about financial stability and job security.

- Despite these challenges, Gen Z is characterized by financial prudence and a desire for financial independence. They are more likely to seek gig work, freelance opportunities, and entrepreneurial ventures to supplement their income.

6. Technology Adoption:

- Gen Z's relationship with technology is distinctive. They are not only consumers of digital content but also creators. Platforms like TikTok, YouTube, and Instagram are popular among Gen Z for content creation and sharing.

- Their proficiency with technology extends to using apps for various aspects of life, including education, finance, health, and entertainment.

Gen Z represents a generation defined by its digital upbringing, global connectivity, and commitment to values such as inclusivity and sustainability. Their unique characteristics and diverse demographic profile position them as a significant influence on societal trends, consumer behavior, and future innovations. Understanding Gen Z's definition and demographics is crucial for engaging with this generation effectively and anticipating their impact on the world.

Key Characteristics of the Gen Z Psychology

Understanding the key characteristics of Gen Z psychology is essential for gaining insights into their behavior, motivations, and interactions. This chapter delves into the distinctive psychological traits that define Gen Z, offering a comprehensive analysis of their cognitive processes, emotional tendencies, and social dynamics.

Digital Natives

Gen Z is the first generation to be born into a world where digital technology is seamlessly integrated into everyday life. From a young age, they have been exposed to smartphones, tablets, and computers, shaping their cognitive development and interaction patterns.

1. Cognitive Agility:

- Gen Z is adept at multitasking and processing information from multiple sources simultaneously. This cognitive agility is a result of their constant engagement with digital devices and platforms, allowing them to quickly switch between tasks and adapt to new information.

2. Information Savvy:

- Growing up with the internet has made Gen Z highly skilled at finding, evaluating, and utilizing information. They are proficient in using search engines, social media, and other online resources to gather data and form opinions.

Global Connectivity

The internet has made the world more interconnected than ever before, and Gen Z has been at the forefront of this global connectivity. They are more exposed to diverse cultures, ideas, and perspectives, which shapes their worldview and social interactions.

1. Cultural Awareness:

- Gen Z's exposure to different cultures through social media and digital content has fostered a deep sense of cultural awareness and appreciation for diversity. They are more likely to embrace and celebrate differences in race, ethnicity, and nationality.

2. Global Citizenship:

- This generation sees themselves as global citizens, often engaging in discussions and activism related to global issues such as climate change, human rights, and social justice. Their global perspective influences their values and actions.

Value-Driven

Gen Z is characterized by a strong sense of values and principles, often centered around social justice, inclusivity, and environmental sustainability. These values are deeply ingrained in their psychology and influence their behavior and decision-making.

1. Social Justice Advocates:

- Gen Z is highly attuned to issues of social justice, including racial equality, gender rights, and LGBTQ+ rights. They are vocal advocates for these causes, using social media platforms to raise awareness and drive change.

2. Environmental Consciousness:

- Environmental sustainability is a significant concern for Gen Z. They are more likely to support eco-friendly practices and products, participate in environmental activism, and hold companies accountable for their environmental impact.

Instant Gratification

The digital age has fostered a culture of instant gratification, where information, entertainment, and services are available at the click of a button. Gen Z, having grown up in this environment, often expects immediate results and responses.

1. Expectation of Speed:

- Gen Z's expectation of quick responses extends to various aspects of life, including communication, customer service, and content consumption. They are less tolerant of delays and inefficiencies.

2. Impact on Patience and Focus:

- The constant availability of instant gratification can impact Gen Z's patience and attention span. They may find it challenging to engage in activities that require prolonged focus and delayed rewards.

Entrepreneurial Spirit

Gen Z exhibits a strong entrepreneurial spirit, driven by a desire for financial independence and creative expression. This generation is leveraging digital tools and platforms to create businesses, content, and innovative solutions.

1. Digital Entrepreneurs:

- Many Gen Z individuals are starting their own businesses or monetizing their skills through digital platforms. From e-commerce stores to YouTube channels, they are exploring various avenues to generate income and build their brands.

2. Innovation and Creativity:

- Gen Z values creativity and innovation, often seeking out new ways to solve problems and express themselves. They are not afraid to challenge the status quo and experiment with unconventional ideas.

Mental Health Awareness

Mental health is a critical issue for Gen Z, with many experiencing high levels of stress, anxiety, and depression. This generation is more open about discussing mental health issues and seeking help when needed.

1. Openness and Vulnerability:

- Gen Z is more likely to share their mental health struggles openly, both online and offline. They value vulnerability and authenticity, creating supportive communities where individuals can express their feelings and seek support.

2. Demand for Mental Health Resources:

- There is a growing demand for mental health resources and services among Gen Z. They are advocating for better access to mental health care and greater awareness of mental health issues in society.

The key characteristics of Gen Z psychology are shaped by their unique experiences and the digital environment in which they have grown up. As digital natives with a global perspective, strong values, and an entrepreneurial spirit, Gen Z is poised to make a significant impact on society. Understanding these psychological traits is essential for engaging with this generation effectively and anticipating their influence on future trends.

Digital Natives: The First True Internet Generation

Gen Z, born approximately between 1997 and 2012, represents the first true generation of digital natives. Unlike previous generations, Gen Z has grown up in an environment where digital technology and the internet are deeply integrated into everyday life. This chapter explores the psychological implications of being digital natives, examining how constant connectivity, access to information, and digital interactions shape their cognitive and emotional development.

Early Exposure to Technology

From a young age, Gen Z has been immersed in digital technology. Smartphones, tablets, and computers have been ubiquitous in their lives, providing them with instant access to information, entertainment, and social interactions.

1. Cognitive Development:

   - The early and frequent use of digital devices has influenced the cognitive development of Gen Z. They have developed strong visual-spatial skills, enhanced by the interactive nature of digital media. This generation is adept at navigating complex interfaces and multitasking across various digital platforms.

2. Learning and Information Processing:

- Gen Z's learning style is heavily influenced by their digital experiences. They prefer interactive and multimedia content, which makes learning more engaging and dynamic. The ability to access information quickly has made them proficient in finding, evaluating, and synthesizing data from multiple sources.

Constant Connectivity

Being constantly connected to the internet has profound implications for how Gen Z interacts with the world. This connectivity shapes their social interactions, emotional experiences, and even their sense of identity.

1. Social Interactions:

- Social media platforms such as Instagram, Snapchat, and TikTok play a central role in Gen Z's social life. These platforms facilitate constant communication and allow them to maintain relationships with peers across the globe. The virtual nature of these interactions can both enhance and complicate social dynamics.

2. Emotional Experiences:

- The digital landscape offers Gen Z immediate emotional gratification. Likes, comments, and shares on social media provide instant feedback, which can boost self-esteem but also lead to increased anxiety and stress. The pressure to maintain an online persona can impact their emotional well-being.

3. Identity Formation:

- The internet allows Gen Z to explore and express their identities in diverse ways. Online communities and platforms provide spaces for self-expression and identity exploration, helping them connect with like-minded individuals and causes. This can foster a strong sense of belonging but also exposes them to potential negative influences.

Digital Literacy and Information Savvy

Gen Z's proficiency with digital technology extends beyond mere usage; they are also highly literate in navigating and utilizing digital information. This digital literacy impacts their educational and professional pursuits.

1. Educational Impact:

- Gen Z leverages digital tools for education, from online research to e-learning platforms. They are comfortable with digital textbooks, video tutorials, and educational apps, which enhance their learning experiences and provide opportunities for personalized education.

2. Professional Skills:

- In the professional realm, Gen Z's digital literacy translates into valuable skills. They are proficient in using productivity software, digital collaboration tools, and social media for professional networking. These skills make them well-suited for the modern workforce, which increasingly relies on digital technologies.

Challenges of Digital Nativism

While being digital natives offers numerous advantages, it also presents unique challenges for Gen Z. These challenges include issues related to mental health, attention span, and the digital divide.

1. Mental Health Concerns:

- The constant connectivity and pressure to maintain an online presence can contribute to mental health issues such as anxiety, depression, and loneliness. Gen Z is more likely to experience cyberbullying and online harassment, which can have significant psychological impacts.

2. Attention Span and Focus:

- The fast-paced digital environment has implications for Gen Z's attention span. They are accustomed to quick, bite-sized content and may find it challenging to engage in activities that require sustained focus and concentration. This can impact their academic performance and productivity.

3. Digital Divide:

- Despite their proficiency with technology, not all Gen Z individuals have equal access to digital resources.

Socioeconomic disparities can lead to a digital divide, where some members of this generation lack access to the necessary tools and connectivity for education and personal development.

Positive Aspects of Digital Nativism

Despite the challenges, being digital natives also brings several positive aspects that contribute to Gen Z's unique strengths and capabilities.

1. Adaptability and Resilience:

- Gen Z is highly adaptable, able to quickly learn and adjust to new technologies and environments. This resilience is a valuable trait in an ever-changing digital landscape and prepares them to navigate future technological advancements.

2. Creativity and Innovation:

- The digital age has fostered a culture of creativity and innovation among Gen Z. They use digital tools to create content, develop new ideas, and engage in entrepreneurial ventures. This creative spirit drives them to explore new possibilities and push boundaries.

3. Global Awareness and Advocacy:

- Gen Z's global connectivity enhances their awareness of social and environmental issues. They use digital platforms to advocate for causes they care about, from climate change to social justice. This activism is a testament to their commitment to making a positive impact on the world.

As the first true digital natives, Gen Z's psychology is profoundly shaped by their digital upbringing. Their early exposure to technology, constant connectivity, and digital literacy define their cognitive and emotional development, social interactions, and professional skills. While they face unique challenges, their adaptability, creativity, and global awareness position them as a generation poised to influence the future in significant ways. Understanding these key characteristics is essential for engaging with Gen Z effectively and harnessing their potential for positive change.

CHAPTER 02

THE DIGITAL LANDSCAPTE OF GEN Z

The Rise of Social Media

Social media has profoundly impacted Generation Z, shaping their communication, social interactions, and worldview. As the first generation to grow up with social media as a central part of their lives, Gen Z's relationship with these platforms is unique and multifaceted. This chapter explores the rise of social media, its influence on Gen Z, and how it continues to evolve.

The Emergence of Social Media Platforms

Social media's journey began in the early 2000s with platforms like MySpace and Friendster. However, it was the advent of Facebook in 2004 that truly revolutionized social networking. Following Facebook's success, a plethora of social media platforms emerged, each catering to different aspects of online interaction.

1. Facebook:

- Initially popular among college students, Facebook quickly expanded its user base across all age groups. For Gen Z, Facebook served as an introduction to social networking but has since become less popular compared to other platforms.

2. Instagram:

- Launched in 2010, Instagram captivated Gen Z with its focus on visual content. The platform's emphasis on photos and videos, coupled with features like Stories and IGTV, made it a favorite among young users for sharing moments and expressing creativity.

3. Snapchat:

- Snapchat, introduced in 2011, revolutionized the way Gen Z communicates. Its ephemeral messaging and multimedia features resonated with the generation's desire for quick, playful interactions. Snapchat's filters and lenses also added a fun, creative dimension to social media.

4. Twitter:

- Although Twitter, launched in 2006, was initially popular for microblogging among Millennials, Gen Z has also embraced the platform for its real-time updates and succinct communication style. Twitter is often used by Gen Z to follow news, trends, and public figures.

5. TikTok:

- TikTok, launched internationally in 2018, has quickly become one of the most popular social media platforms among Gen Z. Its short-form video content, algorithm-driven feed, and emphasis on creativity and virality have made it a cultural phenomenon.

6. Other Platforms:

- Platforms like YouTube, Reddit, and Discord also play significant roles in Gen Z's social media landscape. YouTube serves as a major source of entertainment and information, while Reddit and Discord provide community-driven spaces for niche interests and discussions.

Social Media and Communication

Social media has transformed the way Gen Z communicates, providing diverse platforms for sharing, connecting, and expressing themselves. This transformation is characterized by immediacy, visual emphasis, and a blend of public and private interactions.

1. Immediacy and Real-Time Interaction:

- Social media enables instant communication, allowing Gen Z to share updates, thoughts, and experiences in real time. This immediacy fosters a sense of closeness and continuous connection with peers.

2. Visual Emphasis:

- Platforms like Instagram, Snapchat, and TikTok prioritize visual content, making photos and videos the primary modes of communication. Gen Z uses visuals to convey emotions, tell stories, and create a personal brand.

3. Public and Private Blending:

- Social media blurs the lines between public and private interactions. Gen Z navigates this blend by curating their public persona on platforms like Instagram while engaging in more private, ephemeral conversations on Snapchat and direct messaging.

Social Media and Identity

For Gen Z, social media is not just a communication tool but also a platform for identity exploration and expression. It offers a space for them to present different facets of themselves, experiment with identities, and find like-minded communities.

1. Curated Self-Presentation:

- Social media allows Gen Z to curate their online persona carefully. They can choose what to share, how to present themselves, and what narrative to build around their identity. This curated self-presentation can influence self-esteem and social validation.

2. Exploration of Interests and Identities:

- Platforms like TikTok and Instagram expose Gen Z to diverse content, communities, and subcultures. This exposure facilitates the exploration of interests, hobbies, and identities, helping them discover and connect with their passions and values.

3. Community and Belonging:

- Social media provides a sense of community and belonging. Gen Z can find and join groups that share their interests, beliefs, and experiences. These online communities offer support, validation, and a platform for collective action.

Social Media and Mental Health

While social media offers numerous benefits, it also poses challenges to Gen Z's mental health. The pressures of online presence, comparison, and cyberbullying can impact their psychological well-being.

1. Pressure to Perform and Conform:

- The desire for social validation and approval can lead to pressure to perform and conform to certain standards. This pressure can result in anxiety, stress, and a fear of missing out (FOMO).

2. Comparison and Self-Esteem:

- Constant exposure to curated, idealized representations of others' lives can lead to unhealthy comparisons. Gen Z may struggle with self-esteem issues as they compare their real lives to the seemingly perfect lives portrayed on social media.

3. Cyberbullying and Online Harassment:

- Social media can also be a platform for cyberbullying and online harassment. Negative interactions and harmful comments can have serious psychological impacts, including depression and anxiety.

Social Media as a Platform for Activism

Gen Z leverages social media as a powerful tool for activism and advocacy. They use these platforms to raise awareness, mobilize support, and drive social change on issues they care about.

1. Raising Awareness:

- Social media enables Gen Z to raise awareness about social, environmental, and political issues. Hashtags, viral campaigns, and informational posts help spread messages and educate others.

2. Mobilizing Support:

- Platforms like Twitter and Instagram are used to organize protests, fundraisers, and petitions. Gen Z's ability to mobilize support quickly and efficiently makes them effective advocates for change.

3. Driving Social Change:

- Gen Z's activism on social media has led to tangible social change. They hold corporations and public figures accountable, push for policy changes, and promote social justice movements.

The Evolution of Social Media

Social media continues to evolve, and Gen Z is at the forefront of this evolution. Emerging trends and technologies will shape the future of social media and how Gen Z interacts with it.

1. Augmented Reality (AR) and Virtual Reality (VR):

- AR and VR are becoming more integrated into social media platforms, offering immersive experiences and new ways to interact. Gen Z is likely to adopt these technologies enthusiastically.

2. Niche and Interest-Based Platforms:

- Niche platforms catering to specific interests and communities are gaining popularity. Gen Z seeks spaces where they can connect with others who share their passions and values.

3. Privacy and Security:

- Concerns about privacy and data security are growing. Social media platforms will need to address these concerns to maintain Gen Z's trust and engagement.

The rise of social media has fundamentally shaped the psychology and behavior of Generation Z. As digital natives, they navigate a complex landscape of communication, identity, mental health, and activism through these platforms. Understanding the nuances of Gen Z's relationship with social media is essential for engaging with this generation effectively and anticipating the future of digital interaction.

Social media is not just a tool for Gen Z; it is an integral part of their lives, influencing how they see the world and themselves.

Video Content: YouTube, TikTok, and Beyond

Video content has become a dominant force in the digital lives of Generation Z. Platforms like YouTube and TikTok, along with emerging video-centric platforms, have revolutionized how this generation consumes, creates, and interacts with content. This chapter delves into the significance of video content for Gen Z, exploring the impact of YouTube and TikTok, the rise of short-form videos, and the broader implications for communication, education, and entertainment.

The Dominance of YouTube

YouTube, launched in 2005, has grown into a behemoth of video content, hosting billions of videos across every conceivable genre. For Gen Z, YouTube serves as a primary source of entertainment, education, and social connection.

1. Entertainment Hub:

- YouTube offers an endless array of entertainment options, from music videos and vlogs to gaming streams and comedy sketches. Gen Z spends a significant amount of time on YouTube, watching their favorite creators and discovering new content.

2. Educational Resource:

- YouTube is also a valuable educational tool for Gen Z. The platform hosts countless tutorials, lectures, and how-to videos, making it a go-to resource for learning new skills and gaining knowledge. Educational channels cover topics from academic subjects to practical life skills.

3. Content Creation and Influence:

- Many Gen Z individuals are not just passive consumers of YouTube content; they are also active creators. Aspiring YouTubers use the platform to share their talents, opinions, and lifestyles, often building substantial followings. Influencers on YouTube have significant sway over Gen Z's preferences and behaviors.

The Phenomenon of TikTok

TikTok, launched internationally in 2018, has quickly become a cultural phenomenon, particularly among Gen Z. Its unique format and algorithm-driven content discovery have set it apart from other social media platforms.

1. Short-Form Video Content:

- TikTok's short-form video format, with clips ranging from 15 seconds to a minute, caters to Gen Z's preference for quick, engaging content. The platform's emphasis on creativity and trends encourages users to participate in challenges, dances, and memes.

2. Algorithmic Content Discovery:

- TikTok's powerful algorithm tailors the content feed to each user's preferences, ensuring a highly personalized and addictive viewing experience. This algorithm-driven discovery keeps users engaged and constantly exposed to new content.

3. Viral Trends and Challenges:

- TikTok is known for its viral trends and challenges, which spread rapidly across the platform. These trends often transcend the digital realm, influencing music charts, fashion, and even language. Gen Z actively participates in creating and propagating these trends.

4. Community and Connection:

- Despite its vast user base, TikTok fosters a sense of community through niche interests and subcultures. Gen Z finds and connects with like-minded individuals, creating a sense of belonging and shared identity.

The Appeal of Short-Form Videos

The rise of platforms like TikTok highlights the growing appeal of short-form video content. This format aligns with Gen Z's fast-paced, multitasking lifestyle, offering quick bursts of entertainment and information.

1. Brevity and Impact:

- Short-form videos capture attention quickly and convey messages succinctly. This brevity is particularly appealing to Gen Z, who often seek instant gratification and rapid consumption of content.

2. Creativity and Innovation:

- The constraints of short-form video encourage creativity and innovation. Content creators use clever editing, visual effects, and storytelling techniques to make an impact within a limited time frame.

3. Accessibility and Engagement:

- Short-form videos are easy to create and share, lowering the barrier to entry for content creation. Gen Z's engagement with these videos is high, as they can quickly like, comment, and share content across their networks.

The Role of Video Content in Communication

Video content has transformed how Gen Z communicates, offering dynamic and immersive ways to express themselves and connect with others.

1. Visual Storytelling:

- Video allows for rich visual storytelling, combining images, sound, and motion to convey emotions and narratives. Gen Z uses video to document their lives, share experiences, and communicate complex ideas effectively.

2. Authenticity and Relatability:

- Video content often feels more authentic and relatable compared to text or static images. Gen Z values genuine expressions and personal connections, which video facilitates through direct, unfiltered communication.

3. Interactive and Live Content:

- Platforms like Instagram Live, YouTube Live, and Twitch offer real-time interaction through live streaming. Gen Z engages with live content to participate in events, interact with creators, and join discussions as they unfold.

Video Content in Education

Video content plays a crucial role in the educational experiences of Gen Z, offering flexible, engaging, and diverse learning opportunities.

1. Online Tutorials and Courses:

- Platforms like YouTube and educational sites like Khan Academy provide extensive libraries of tutorials and courses. Gen Z uses these resources to supplement traditional education and learn at their own pace.

2. Visual and Interactive Learning:

- Video enhances learning by providing visual and interactive elements. Educational videos often incorporate animations, diagrams, and real-world demonstrations, making complex concepts easier to understand.

3. Peer Learning and Collaboration:

- Gen Z often turns to video content for peer learning and collaboration. They watch videos created by their peers, share insights, and collaborate on projects using video as a medium for communication and presentation.

The Broader Implications for Entertainment

Video content has redefined entertainment for Gen Z, blending traditional media with user-generated content and interactive experiences.

1. Streaming Services:

- Streaming services like Netflix, Hulu, and Disney+ offer on-demand access to a vast array of movies, TV shows, and documentaries. Gen Z consumes a significant portion of their entertainment through these platforms, often binge-watching series.

2. Gaming and Esports:

- Video content extends to gaming and esports, where platforms like Twitch and YouTube Gaming provide live streams and recorded gameplay. Gen Z engages with gaming content as both players and spectators, participating in a growing esports culture.

3. Interactive and Immersive Experiences:

- Emerging technologies like virtual reality (VR) and augmented reality (AR) are creating new avenues for interactive and immersive video experiences. Gen Z is at the forefront of adopting these technologies, exploring new ways to interact with digital content.

Video content, exemplified by platforms like YouTube and TikTok, is a cornerstone of Gen Z's digital landscape. Its dominance reflects the generation's preference for dynamic, engaging, and authentic communication. As video content continues to evolve, its impact on Gen Z's communication, education, and entertainment will only deepen. Understanding the significance of video content for Gen Z is essential for anyone looking to connect with this influential generation and anticipate the future of digital media.

The Influence of Digital Influencers and Content Creators

Digital influencers and content creators have become central figures in the lives of Generation Z, shaping their tastes, behaviors, and perceptions in profound ways. This chapter explores the rise of digital influencers, their impact on Gen Z, and the broader implications for marketing, identity, and social dynamics.

The Rise of Digital Influencers

Digital influencers are individuals who have built a significant following on social media platforms through their content creation. These influencers can range from celebrities and industry experts to everyday people who have gained popularity within specific niches.

1. Types of Influencers:

- Macro-Influencers: These are individuals with a vast following, often in the millions. They include celebrities, well-known public figures, and top-tier content creators.

- Micro-Influencers: These influencers have a smaller, yet highly engaged following, typically ranging from 10,000 to 100,000 followers. They often cater to niche audiences and are considered more relatable and authentic.

- Nano-Influencers: With followers in the range of 1,000 to 10,000, nano-influencers have highly dedicated and engaged audiences. They often focus on very specific interests or communities.

2. Platform-Specific Influence:

- YouTube: Known for long-form content, YouTube influencers create videos ranging from vlogs and tutorials to reviews and entertainment content. Their influence extends to shaping opinions, promoting products, and even educating their audience.

- Instagram: Instagram influencers use visual content, such as photos and short videos, to engage their followers. They are particularly influential in fashion, lifestyle, and beauty sectors.

- TikTok: TikTok influencers thrive on creating short, engaging videos that often go viral. Their content includes dances, challenges, comedic skits, and educational snippets, appealing to Gen Z's preference for quick, entertaining content.

- Twitch: Focused on live streaming, particularly in gaming, Twitch influencers interact with their audience in real-time, fostering a strong sense of community and immediacy.

The Impact on Gen Z

Digital influencers hold significant sway over Gen Z's preferences, behaviors, and worldviews. Their impact can be seen across various aspects of Gen Z's lives, from consumer choices to personal identity.

1. Consumer Behavior:

- Brand Endorsements and Product Reviews: Influencers often collaborate with brands to promote products. Gen Z values these endorsements, considering them more authentic and trustworthy compared to traditional advertisements. Product reviews by influencers can significantly impact Gen Z's purchasing decisions.

- Trends and Fads: Influencers are trendsetters, often initiating and popularizing new trends and fads. Whether it's a fashion style, a viral challenge, or a new app, influencers' recommendations quickly gain traction among Gen Z.

2. Identity and Self-Expression:

- Role Models and Inspiration: Influencers serve as role models, providing inspiration and guidance on various aspects of life, from career advice to personal development. Gen Z looks up to influencers who reflect their values and aspirations.

- Self-Representation: Influencers showcase diverse identities and lifestyles, encouraging Gen Z to embrace and express their own unique identities. This visibility fosters a sense of acceptance and belonging among Gen Z.

3. Social and Political Engagement:

- Advocacy and Activism: Many influencers use their platforms to advocate for social and political causes. Gen Z, who values social justice and activism, is inspired by influencers who speak out on issues such as climate change, racial equality, and mental health.

- Community Building: Influencers create and nurture communities around shared interests and values. These communities offer support, connection, and a sense of belonging for Gen Z, who often feel isolated or disconnected in the physical world.

The Broader Implications for Marketing

The influence of digital influencers has transformed the marketing landscape, prompting brands to adapt their strategies to engage Gen Z effectively.

1. Influencer Marketing:

- Strategic Partnerships: Brands collaborate with influencers to reach their target audience in an authentic and relatable manner. Influencer marketing campaigns are designed to align with the influencer's content style and audience preferences, ensuring genuine engagement.

- User-Generated Content: Influencers encourage their followers to create and share content related to the brand, amplifying the campaign's reach and impact. This user-generated content fosters a sense of community and involvement among consumers.

2. Authenticity and Transparency:

- Genuine Endorsements: Gen Z values authenticity and can easily detect insincere endorsements. Successful influencer marketing relies on genuine recommendations that resonate with the influencer's personal brand and audience.

- Transparency in Partnerships: Disclosure of sponsored content is crucial for maintaining trust. Influencers who are transparent about their partnerships and honest in their reviews are more likely to retain credibility with their audience.

Challenges and Ethical Considerations

While the influence of digital influencers is significant, it also presents challenges and ethical considerations that need to be addressed.

1. Mental Health and Well-Being:

- Pressure and Comparison: The curated and often idealized lives of influencers can create pressure and unrealistic expectations for Gen Z. This comparison can lead to issues such as anxiety, low self-esteem, and depression.

- Burnout Among Influencers: The constant demand for content creation and maintaining an online presence can lead to burnout among influencers. This stress can impact their mental health and the quality of their content.

2. Authenticity vs. Commercialization:

- Balancing Authenticity: As influencers grow and collaborate with brands, maintaining authenticity becomes challenging. Over-commercialization can erode trust and alienate their audience.

- Ethical Endorsements: Influencers have a responsibility to endorse products and brands that align with their values and do not exploit or mislead their audience.

3. Diversity and Inclusion:

- Representation: Ensuring diverse representation among influencers is essential for inclusivity. Brands and platforms must support influencers from various backgrounds and promote a wide range of voices.

- Addressing Bias: Platforms and brands need to address biases in their algorithms and marketing strategies to ensure fair and equitable opportunities for all influencers.

The Future of Influencer Culture

The future of digital influencers and content creators will continue to evolve, driven by technological advancements, changing consumer behaviors, and emerging platforms.

1. Technological Innovations:

- Augmented Reality (AR) and Virtual Reality (VR): AR and VR technologies will create new opportunities for immersive and interactive content. Influencers will leverage these technologies to offer unique experiences and engage their audience in novel ways.

- Artificial Intelligence (AI): AI-powered tools will enhance content creation, personalization, and audience engagement. Influencers will use AI to analyze trends, optimize content, and connect with their followers more effectively.

2. Evolving Platforms:

- New Social Media Platforms: As new platforms emerge, influencers will adapt and explore these spaces to reach their audience. The dynamic nature of social media will continue to offer fresh opportunities for content creation and engagement.

- Niche Communities: Influencers will increasingly focus on niche communities, creating content tailored to specific interests and demographics. These specialized audiences will foster deeper connections and higher engagement.

3. Sustainable and Ethical Practices:

- Responsible Influencing: The emphasis on sustainability and ethics will shape the future of influencer culture. Influencers and brands will prioritize responsible practices, promoting products and messages that align with social and environmental values.

- Transparency and Accountability: Greater transparency and accountability will be demanded from influencers and brands. This shift will lead to more authentic and trustworthy content, reinforcing the bond between influencers and their audience.

Digital influencers and content creators hold a powerful influence over Generation Z, shaping their consumer behaviors, identities, and social dynamics. As the digital landscape continues to evolve, the role of influencers will expand, presenting both opportunities and challenges. Understanding the impact of digital influencers on Gen Z is crucial for navigating the complexities of modern marketing, fostering authentic connections, and promoting responsible and ethical practices in the digital age.

CHAPTER 03

PSYCHOLOGICAL PROFILE OF GEN Z

Cognitive and Emotional Development

Generation Z, born approximately between 1997 and 2012, is the first generation to grow up in a world where digital technology is ubiquitous. This unique environment has profoundly influenced their cognitive and emotional development. This chapter explores the key aspects of Gen Z's cognitive and emotional growth, highlighting how their upbringing in a digitally connected world has shaped their thinking patterns, learning styles, and emotional well-being.

Cognitive Development

The cognitive development of Gen Z is marked by their early and constant exposure to digital technology. This exposure has resulted in distinct cognitive traits that differentiate them from previous generations.

1. Information Processing:

- Multitasking: Gen Z is adept at multitasking, often engaging with multiple screens and tasks simultaneously. This ability to switch rapidly between different activities reflects their proficiency in handling diverse streams of information.

- Rapid Information Consumption: Growing up with the internet has conditioned Gen Z to consume information quickly. They are skilled at skimming content and identifying key points, allowing them to process large volumes of information efficiently.

2. Learning Styles:

- Visual and Interactive Learning: Gen Z prefers visual and interactive learning methods. They are drawn to content that includes videos, infographics, and interactive elements, which make learning more engaging and effective.

- Self-Directed Learning: The availability of online resources has fostered a culture of self-directed learning among Gen Z. They often seek out information independently, using platforms like YouTube, Khan Academy, and online forums to supplement their education.

3. Critical Thinking and Problem Solving:

- Access to Diverse Perspectives: The internet provides Gen Z with access to a wide range of perspectives and information sources. This exposure enhances their critical thinking skills, as they learn to evaluate and synthesize diverse viewpoints.

- Innovative Problem Solving: Gen Z's familiarity with digital tools and platforms encourages innovative problem-solving. They are more likely to use technology creatively to address challenges and find solutions.

4. Attention Span:

- Shortened Attention Span: The fast-paced digital environment has contributed to a shorter attention span among Gen Z. They are accustomed to quick, bite-sized content and may struggle with prolonged focus on a single task.

- Adaptability: Despite their shorter attention spans, Gen Z is highly adaptable. They can quickly shift their focus and adapt to new information or changing circumstances, making them resilient in dynamic environments.

Emotional Development

The emotional development of Gen Z is deeply intertwined with their digital experiences. Social media, online communities, and constant connectivity have influenced their emotional well-being and social interactions.

1. Social Media and Emotional Well-Being:

- Positive Reinforcement: Social media platforms provide instant feedback through likes, comments, and shares. This positive reinforcement can boost self-esteem and provide a sense of validation.

- Comparison and Pressure: However, the curated nature of social media can also lead to negative comparisons and pressure to conform to idealized standards. Gen Z may experience anxiety and low self-esteem as they compare their lives to the seemingly perfect lives of others.

2. Mental Health Awareness:

- Openness to Discuss Mental Health: Gen Z is more open about discussing mental health issues compared to previous generations. They are likely to seek help and share their experiences openly, reducing the stigma around mental health.

- Access to Resources: The internet offers a wealth of resources for mental health support, from online therapy services to mental health apps. Gen Z utilizes these resources to manage their emotional well-being proactively.

3. Identity Formation:

- Exploration and Expression: Digital platforms provide spaces for Gen Z to explore and express their identities. Online communities, social media profiles, and content creation allow them to experiment with different aspects of their identity in a supportive environment.

- Belonging and Community: The ability to connect with like-minded individuals online fosters a sense of belonging and community. Gen Z finds support and acceptance in digital communities, which plays a crucial role in their emotional development.

4. Resilience and Coping Mechanisms:

- Digital Coping Strategies: Gen Z uses digital tools as coping mechanisms for stress and anxiety. Whether it's through mindfulness apps, virtual support groups, or engaging in hobbies online, they leverage technology to manage their emotional health.

- Adaptability to Change: Growing up in a rapidly changing digital world has made Gen Z resilient and adaptable. They are more comfortable with change and uncertainty, which helps them cope with emotional challenges.

Challenges and Opportunities

While the digital environment offers numerous benefits for Gen Z's cognitive and emotional development, it also presents unique challenges and opportunities.

1. Digital Overload and Burnout:

- Constant Connectivity: The constant connectivity can lead to digital overload and burnout. Gen Z may struggle to disconnect and find balance between their online and offline lives.

- Strategies for Balance: Encouraging healthy digital habits, such as setting boundaries and taking regular breaks, can help mitigate the risks of digital overload. Promoting offline activities and face-to-face interactions is also essential.

2. Cyberbullying and Online Harassment:

- Prevalence of Cyberbullying: The anonymity and reach of the internet can facilitate cyberbullying and online harassment. These negative experiences can have severe emotional impacts on Gen Z.

- Support and Intervention: Providing support and intervention strategies, such as digital literacy education and mental health resources, can help Gen Z navigate and address these challenges.

3. Educational and Professional Development:

- Leveraging Digital Skills: Gen Z's digital skills offer opportunities for educational and professional development. They can leverage their familiarity with technology to excel in fields such as digital marketing, coding, and content creation.

- Lifelong Learning: Emphasizing the importance of lifelong learning and continuous skill development can empower Gen Z to adapt to the evolving job market and technological advancements.

Gen Z's cognitive and emotional development is profoundly influenced by their digital upbringing. Their unique cognitive traits, such as multitasking and rapid information processing, along with their emotional experiences shaped by social media and online communities, define their psychological profile. Understanding these aspects of Gen Z's development is crucial for parents, educators, and employers to support their growth and well-being effectively. As digital natives, Gen Z has the potential to navigate and thrive in a dynamic and interconnected world, leveraging their strengths and addressing the challenges posed by their digital environment.

Social Media and Mental Health

The relationship between social media and mental health is a complex and multifaceted one, especially for Generation Z. As the first generation to grow up with pervasive access to social media platforms, Gen Z's mental health is significantly influenced by their online experiences. This chapter delves into the positive and negative impacts of social media on Gen Z's mental health, exploring both the benefits and challenges they face in navigating their digital lives.

The Positive Impact of Social Media on Mental Health

Despite the often-highlighted negative aspects, social media can also offer several positive benefits for the mental health of Gen Z.

1. Social Connection and Support:

- Maintaining Relationships: Social media platforms enable Gen Z to maintain connections with friends and family, regardless of geographical distance. This continuous communication helps sustain relationships and provides a sense of closeness.

- Finding Supportive Communities: Social media offers a space for Gen Z to find and join communities of like-minded individuals. These communities can provide emotional support, validation, and a sense of belonging, especially for those who may feel isolated in their offline lives.

2. Mental Health Awareness and Education:

- Access to Information: Social media is a valuable source of information on mental health. Gen Z can access educational content, resources, and expert advice on managing mental health issues.

- Reducing Stigma: The open discussion of mental health on social media helps reduce stigma. Influencers and peers sharing their mental health journeys encourage Gen Z to seek help and talk about their struggles without fear of judgment.

3. Opportunities for Self-Expression and Creativity:

- Creative Outlets: Platforms like Instagram, TikTok, and YouTube provide Gen Z with creative outlets to express themselves. Engaging in creative activities can be therapeutic and contribute to improved mental well-being.

- Building Identity: Social media allows Gen Z to explore and express their identities. This process of self-discovery and expression can foster self-confidence and a positive self-image.

The Negative Impact of Social Media on Mental Health

While social media offers numerous benefits, it also poses significant challenges to the mental health of Gen Z.

1. Comparison and Self-Esteem:

- Curated Perfection: Social media often showcases curated, idealized versions of people's lives. Gen Z may compare themselves to these unrealistic portrayals, leading to feelings of inadequacy and low self-esteem.

- Pressure to Perform: The pressure to gain likes, comments, and followers can create a constant need for validation. This external validation can become a primary source of self-worth, impacting mental health when it is not achieved.

2. Cyberbullying and Online Harassment:

- Prevalence of Cyberbullying: The anonymity and reach of social media can facilitate cyberbullying and harassment. Negative interactions, such as mean comments, spreading rumors, and exclusion, can have severe emotional impacts on Gen Z.

- Emotional Consequences: Victims of cyberbullying may experience anxiety, depression, and even suicidal thoughts. The pervasive nature of social media means that these negative experiences can follow individuals everywhere, contributing to ongoing distress.

3. Addiction and Distraction:

- Social Media Addiction: The design of social media platforms encourages prolonged use, leading to potential addiction. Gen Z may find it challenging to disconnect, spending excessive amounts of time online to the detriment of their offline lives.

- Impact on Productivity and Sleep: Excessive social media use can interfere with productivity and sleep patterns. The constant distraction can make it difficult to focus on tasks, while late-night screen time can disrupt sleep, contributing to poor mental health.

Coping Strategies and Interventions

Given the dual impact of social media on mental health, it is crucial to develop coping strategies and interventions to help Gen Z navigate their digital lives healthily.

1. Digital Literacy and Education:

- Teaching Digital Literacy: Educating Gen Z about digital literacy, including how to critically evaluate content and recognize the impact of social media on mental health, can empower them to make informed choices about their online activities.

- Promoting Healthy Habits: Encouraging healthy social media habits, such as setting time limits, taking regular breaks, and engaging in offline activities, can help mitigate the negative impacts of excessive use.

2. Mental Health Resources and Support:

- Access to Professional Help: Providing access to mental health resources, including online therapy and counseling services, can offer crucial support for those struggling with the impact of social media.

- Peer Support Networks: Developing peer support networks, both online and offline, can provide Gen Z with a sense of community and shared understanding. These networks can offer emotional support and practical advice on managing mental health.

3. Platform Accountability and Design:

- Enhancing Platform Safety: Social media platforms have a responsibility to create safer environments for users. This includes implementing robust anti-bullying policies, providing easy access to reporting tools, and offering mental health resources.

- Designing for Well-Being: Platforms can incorporate design features that promote well-being, such as reminders to take breaks, tools for managing screen time, and algorithms that prioritize positive and supportive content.

The Role of Parents, Educators, and Policymakers

Supporting the mental health of Gen Z in the context of social media requires a collaborative effort from parents, educators, and policymakers.

1. Parental Guidance and Monitoring:

- Open Communication: Parents should maintain open lines of communication with their children about their social media use. Discussing the potential impacts and setting healthy boundaries can help manage its influence on mental health.

- Monitoring and Support: While respecting privacy, parents can monitor social media activity to identify signs of distress or harmful interactions. Providing support and intervening when necessary is crucial for protecting mental health.

2. Educational Initiatives:

- Incorporating Mental Health Education: Schools can incorporate mental health education into their curricula, teaching students about the impact of social media and providing strategies for maintaining well-being.

- Training for Educators: Educators should be trained to recognize signs of social media-related distress and provide appropriate support and resources to students.

3. Policy and Regulation:

- Implementing Regulations: Policymakers can implement regulations to protect young users on social media, such as age verification, data privacy protections, and restrictions on harmful content.

- Promoting Research: Supporting research on the impact of social media on mental health can inform evidence-based policies and interventions.

The relationship between social media and the mental health of Generation Z is complex, encompassing both positive and negative aspects. While social media offers opportunities for connection, self-expression, and mental health awareness, it also poses challenges such as comparison, cyberbullying, and addiction. By fostering digital literacy, providing mental health resources, and promoting responsible platform design, we can help Gen Z navigate their digital lives in a way that supports their mental well-being. Understanding and addressing the impact of social media on mental health is essential for ensuring that this generation can thrive in a digital world.

Values and Beliefs: Social Justice, Inclusivity, and Environmental Concerns

Generation Z, born approximately between 1997 and 2012, is characterized by a distinct set of values and beliefs shaped by their unique experiences and upbringing. Central to their worldview are the principles of social justice, inclusivity, and environmental sustainability. This chapter explores these core values and beliefs, examining how they influence Gen Z's behavior, decisions, and aspirations.

Social Justice

Social justice is a cornerstone of Gen Z's values, encompassing a commitment to equality, fairness, and human rights. This generation is particularly attuned to social issues and is proactive in advocating for change.

1. Awareness and Advocacy:

- Exposure to Global Issues: Growing up in a digital age has exposed Gen Z to a wide range of global issues through social media, news, and online communities. They are highly aware of social injustices, including racial inequality, gender discrimination, and LGBTQ+ rights.

- Activism and Advocacy: Gen Z is often at the forefront of social justice movements, participating in protests, signing petitions, and using social media to raise awareness. Platforms like Twitter and Instagram serve as powerful tools for mobilizing support and driving change.

2. Equality and Human Rights:

- Racial and Ethnic Equality: Gen Z places a high value on racial and ethnic equality. They actively oppose racism and support initiatives that promote diversity and inclusion in all aspects of society.

- Gender Equality: Gender equality is another critical issue for Gen Z. They advocate for equal opportunities and rights for all genders, challenging traditional gender roles and stereotypes.

- LGBTQ+ Rights: Gen Z is one of the most LGBTQ+ inclusive generations. They support equal rights for LGBTQ+ individuals and promote acceptance and representation in media, workplaces, and communities.

3. Economic and Social Equity:

- Economic Justice: Economic disparities and inequality are significant concerns for Gen Z. They support policies and initiatives aimed at reducing poverty, improving access to education and healthcare, and ensuring fair wages and working conditions.

- Social Equity: Social equity, including access to resources and opportunities regardless of background, is fundamental to Gen Z's vision of a just society. They advocate for systemic changes to address social inequalities and create a more equitable world.

Inclusivity

Inclusivity is a defining value for Gen Z, who prioritize creating environments where all individuals feel welcome, respected, and valued. This commitment to inclusivity extends to various aspects of their lives, from social interactions to workplace dynamics.

1. Diversity and Representation:

- Cultural and Ethnic Diversity: Gen Z celebrates cultural and ethnic diversity, seeking out and appreciating different perspectives and experiences. They support initiatives that promote diverse representation in media, education, and leadership roles.

- Inclusive Media and Entertainment: Representation in media and entertainment is crucial for Gen Z. They advocate for inclusive storytelling that reflects the diverse world they live in and challenges stereotypes and biases.

2. Accessibility and Accommodation:

- Disability Inclusion: Gen Z is committed to making spaces and opportunities accessible to individuals with disabilities. They support inclusive design, policies, and practices that ensure everyone can participate fully in society.

- Mental Health Awareness: Inclusivity for Gen Z also involves recognizing and accommodating mental health needs. They advocate for mental health awareness, support, and resources in schools, workplaces, and communities.

3. Intersectionality:

- Understanding Intersectionality: Gen Z understands the importance of intersectionality—the interconnected nature of social categorizations such as race, class, and gender as they apply to individuals or groups. They recognize that various forms of discrimination and privilege intersect and impact people's experiences differently.

- Inclusive Activism: Gen Z's activism often incorporates an intersectional approach, addressing multiple issues simultaneously and advocating for comprehensive solutions that consider diverse perspectives and needs.

Environmental Concerns

Environmental sustainability is a critical value for Gen Z, who are deeply concerned about the impact of climate change and environmental degradation. Their commitment to protecting the planet shapes their behavior, choices, and advocacy efforts.

1. Climate Change Awareness:

- Urgency of Climate Action: Gen Z is acutely aware of the urgency of addressing climate change. They recognize the long-term impacts of environmental damage and the need for immediate and substantial action to mitigate its effects.

- Education and Advocacy: Gen Z actively seeks out information on environmental issues and uses their knowledge to advocate for climate action. They participate in climate strikes, support environmental organizations, and use social media to spread awareness.

2. Sustainable Living:

- Eco-Friendly Choices: Gen Z makes conscious choices to live sustainably. This includes reducing waste, recycling, using renewable energy sources, and supporting eco-friendly products and companies.

- Minimalism and Consumption: Many Gen Z individuals adopt minimalist lifestyles, prioritizing experiences over material possessions and making mindful consumption choices that minimize environmental impact.

3. Corporate Responsibility:

- Holding Corporations Accountable: Gen Z expects companies to take responsibility for their environmental impact. They support businesses that implement sustainable practices and are transparent about their efforts to reduce carbon footprints.

- Ethical Consumerism: Gen Z practices ethical consumerism, choosing to support brands and products that align with their environmental values. They use their purchasing power to drive demand for sustainable and ethically produced goods.

4. Policy and Systemic Change:

- Advocating for Policy Changes: Gen Z recognizes that individual actions alone are not enough to address environmental challenges. They advocate for policy changes at local, national, and global levels to enforce environmental protection and sustainability.

- Engaging in Political Processes: Many Gen Z individuals engage in political processes to support candidates and policies that prioritize environmental sustainability. They participate in voting, campaigning, and lobbying efforts to influence change.

The Interconnectedness of Values

For Gen Z, the values of social justice, inclusivity, and environmental concerns are deeply interconnected. They understand that achieving true sustainability requires addressing social inequalities and promoting inclusive practices.

1. Holistic Approach to Advocacy:

- Integrated Activism: Gen Z's activism often integrates multiple issues, recognizing the intersections between social justice, inclusivity, and environmental sustainability. For example, they advocate for climate justice, which addresses the disproportionate impact of climate change on marginalized communities.

- Collaborative Efforts: Gen Z values collaboration and collective action. They work together across different movements and causes, understanding that unified efforts can lead to more significant and lasting change.

2. Personal and Collective Responsibility:

- Individual Actions: Gen Z takes personal responsibility for living according to their values, making choices that reflect their commitment to social justice, inclusivity, and environmental sustainability.

- Collective Impact: They also emphasize the importance of collective responsibility, encouraging others to join in their efforts and recognizing that systemic change requires widespread participation and support.

The values and beliefs of Generation Z, centered around social justice, inclusivity, and environmental concerns, shape their behavior, decisions, and aspirations. Their commitment to these principles drives their activism, influences their consumption choices, and guides their vision for the future. Understanding and supporting these values is essential for engaging with Gen Z effectively and contributing to a more just, inclusive, and sustainable world. As this generation continues to advocate for change, their impact will be felt across various aspects of society, paving the way for a better future for all.

CHAPTER 04

GEN Z'S THINKING PATTERNS

Critical Thinking and Information Processing

Generation Z, born approximately between 1997 and 2012, is distinct in its thinking patterns, particularly in the areas of critical thinking and information processing. Growing up in an era of unprecedented access to information and digital connectivity, Gen Z has developed unique cognitive skills that set them apart from previous generations. This chapter explores how Gen Z approaches critical thinking and information processing, highlighting their strengths, challenges, and the implications for their personal and professional lives.

Critical Thinking in the Digital Age

Critical thinking, the ability to analyze, evaluate, and synthesize information to make informed decisions, is a crucial skill for navigating the complex and information-rich world Gen Z inhabits.

1. Access to Diverse Information:

- Information Abundance: Gen Z has grown up with immediate access to vast amounts of information through the internet. This exposure to diverse perspectives, news sources, and data points has fostered their ability to critically assess information.

- Evaluating Credibility: With the prevalence of misinformation and fake news, Gen Z has become adept at evaluating the credibility of sources. They use various strategies to verify information, such as cross-referencing multiple sources and checking the reliability of authors and websites.

2. Analytical Skills:

- Breaking Down Complex Issues: Gen Z is skilled at breaking down complex issues into manageable parts. They analyze problems from multiple angles, considering various factors and potential outcomes before reaching a conclusion.

- Logical Reasoning: Logical reasoning is a hallmark of Gen Z's critical thinking. They prioritize evidence-based arguments and are cautious of fallacies and biases that can undermine sound reasoning.

3. Open-Mindedness:

- Receptive to New Ideas: Gen Z is generally open-minded and willing to consider new ideas and perspectives. Their exposure to diverse viewpoints online encourages them to remain flexible and adaptable in their thinking.

- Challenging Assumptions: They are not afraid to challenge assumptions and question established norms. This critical approach enables them to innovate and find creative solutions to problems.

Information Processing in the Digital Era

The way Gen Z processes information is deeply influenced by their digital environment. Their cognitive strategies for handling the influx of data and their approach to learning and problem-solving are distinctive.

1. Rapid Information Consumption:

- Skimming and Scanning: Gen Z often skims and scans content to quickly identify key points and relevant information. This skill allows them to process large amounts of data efficiently, though it may sometimes lead to superficial understanding.

- Visual and Multimedia Content: They are drawn to visual and multimedia content, which aids in faster and more engaging information processing. Infographics, videos, and interactive media are particularly effective in capturing their attention and enhancing comprehension.

2. Multitasking and Focus:

- Concurrent Activities: Gen Z is adept at multitasking, often engaging in multiple activities simultaneously, such as browsing social media while doing homework. While this can increase productivity in certain contexts, it may also lead to divided attention and reduced focus on individual tasks.

- Managing Distractions: The constant influx of notifications and digital stimuli requires Gen Z to develop strategies for managing distractions. Techniques such as using focus apps, setting specific times for social media, and creating distraction-free environments help them maintain concentration.

3. Self-Directed Learning:

- Autonomous Information Seeking: Gen Z values autonomy in their learning process. They actively seek out information on their own, using online resources, tutorials, and educational platforms to supplement traditional learning.

- Customized Learning Paths: Digital tools allow Gen Z to customize their learning experiences according to their interests and needs. They can choose the pace, format, and content that best suits their learning style, fostering a more personalized approach to education.

Challenges in Critical Thinking and Information Processing

Despite their strengths, Gen Z faces several challenges in critical thinking and information processing. Addressing these challenges is essential for maximizing their potential.

1. Information Overload:

- Cognitive Overload: The sheer volume of information available can lead to cognitive overload, where the brain becomes overwhelmed by the amount of data it must process. This can result in stress, decision fatigue, and difficulty focusing on essential tasks.

- Prioritizing Information: Learning to prioritize information and focus on what is most relevant is a critical skill. Techniques such as filtering sources, setting clear goals, and using organizational tools can help manage information overload.

2. Quality vs. Quantity:

- Superficial Processing: The tendency to skim and scan can sometimes result in superficial processing of information. Gen Z may need to balance quick consumption with deeper engagement to ensure thorough understanding and retention of complex concepts.

- Depth of Knowledge: Encouraging deeper exploration of subjects and fostering critical discussion can help Gen Z move beyond surface-level knowledge to develop a more profound and comprehensive understanding.

3. Digital Distractions:

- Constant Connectivity: The constant connectivity of the digital world can be a double-edged sword, providing both opportunities and distractions. Gen Z must navigate the challenges of staying focused in an environment filled with digital temptations.

- Developing Discipline: Developing digital discipline, such as setting boundaries for screen time and using productivity tools, can help Gen Z manage distractions and maintain focus on their goals.

Implications for Personal and Professional Development

The critical thinking and information processing skills of Gen Z have significant implications for their personal and professional development. Leveraging these skills can enhance their performance and success in various domains.

1. Academic Achievement:

- Innovative Learning Approaches: Gen Z's ability to process information quickly and critically analyze content positions them well for academic success. Educators can support their learning by incorporating interactive and multimedia content into curricula.

- Critical Inquiry: Promoting critical inquiry and problem-based learning can help Gen Z apply their analytical skills to real-world issues, preparing them for future academic and professional challenges.

2. Career Readiness:

- Adaptability and Innovation: The workforce increasingly values adaptability and innovation, traits that are well-developed in Gen Z. Their critical thinking and information processing abilities enable them to navigate complex problems and contribute to organizational success.

- Digital Proficiency: Gen Z's proficiency with digital tools and technologies is a valuable asset in the modern workplace. Employers can leverage their digital literacy to drive innovation and efficiency.

3. Informed Citizenship:

- Engaged and Informed: Gen Z's critical thinking skills contribute to their engagement as informed citizens. They are more likely to participate in civic activities, stay informed about current events, and advocate for social change.

- Ethical Decision-Making: The ability to critically evaluate information and consider diverse perspectives enhances ethical decision-making. Gen Z can apply these skills to make responsible choices in their personal and professional lives.

Generation Z's critical thinking and information processing skills are shaped by their unique experiences in a digitally connected world. Their ability to analyze, evaluate, and synthesize information sets them apart from previous generations and equips them to navigate the complexities of modern life. While they face challenges such as information overload and digital distractions, their strengths in rapid information consumption, multitasking, and self-directed learning position them for success. Understanding and supporting these cognitive skills is essential for fostering Gen Z's personal and professional development, enabling them to thrive in an ever-evolving digital landscape.

The Impact of Constant Connectivity

Generation Z, born approximately between 1997 and 2012, has grown up in a world where constant connectivity is the norm. This pervasive digital environment, characterized by uninterrupted access to the internet and social media, has significantly influenced their cognitive and emotional development. This chapter explores the impact of constant connectivity on Gen Z, examining its effects on their attention spans, mental health, social interactions, and overall well-being.

Attention Span and Focus

Constant connectivity has had a profound effect on the attention spans and focus of Gen Z. The digital environment, with its rapid flow of information and endless distractions, shapes how they concentrate and process information.

1. Shortened Attention Spans:

- Rapid Information Consumption: Gen Z is accustomed to consuming information in quick, digestible snippets. Social media platforms like TikTok, Twitter, and Instagram encourage short-form content, which has conditioned them to expect immediate gratification and rapid content delivery.

- Multitasking: The ability to switch quickly between tasks and platforms has made Gen Z proficient multitaskers. However, this constant switching can lead to shorter attention spans and difficulties in sustaining focus on a single task for extended periods.

2. Challenges in Deep Work:

- Reduced Ability for Deep Focus: The prevalence of notifications, messages, and alerts can interrupt deep work, making it challenging for Gen Z to engage in prolonged, focused activities such as studying or working on complex projects.

- Cognitive Overload: The barrage of information from multiple sources can lead to cognitive overload, where the brain struggles to process and retain information effectively, resulting in mental fatigue and reduced productivity.

Mental Health and Well-Being

The impact of constant connectivity on mental health is a double-edged sword. While digital connectivity provides opportunities for support and connection, it also poses significant challenges to the mental well-being of Gen Z.

1. Positive Impacts:

- Access to Support Networks: Online communities and social media platforms offer Gen Z access to support networks where they can share their experiences and seek advice. These virtual support systems can provide a sense of belonging and reduce feelings of isolation.

- Mental Health Resources: The internet provides a wealth of mental health resources, including educational content, therapy apps, and online counseling services. Gen Z can access these resources to manage their mental health proactively.

2. Negative Impacts:

- Increased Anxiety and Stress: The pressure to maintain an online presence, gain social validation through likes and comments, and stay updated with the latest trends can contribute to increased anxiety and stress. Fear of missing out (FOMO) exacerbates these feelings, as Gen Z strives to keep up with their peers.

- Cyberbullying and Online Harassment: The anonymity and reach of the internet can facilitate cyberbullying and online harassment, leading to significant emotional distress. Negative online interactions can impact self-esteem, contribute to depression, and even lead to suicidal thoughts.

Social Interactions and Relationships

Constant connectivity has reshaped how Gen Z interacts socially, influencing their relationships and communication styles.

1. Virtual Socialization:

- Online Friendships: Many of Gen Z's social interactions occur online, with virtual friendships playing a significant role in their social lives. These online connections can be as meaningful as offline relationships, providing emotional support and companionship.

- Global Connectivity: The internet enables Gen Z to connect with peers from around the world, fostering cross-cultural understanding and broadening their social horizons. This global connectivity allows them to build diverse and inclusive networks.

2. Communication Styles:

- Preference for Digital Communication: Gen Z often prefers digital communication over face-to-face interactions. Texting, messaging apps, and social media platforms are their primary modes of communication, which can influence their interpersonal skills and comfort with in-person interactions.

- Impact on Social Skills: While digital communication offers convenience, it may also impact the development of social skills such as reading body language, active listening, and conflict resolution. Balancing online and offline interactions is crucial for developing well-rounded social competencies.

Academic and Professional Implications

Constant connectivity has both positive and negative implications for Gen Z's academic and professional development.

1. Academic Benefits:

- Access to Information: The internet provides Gen Z with unprecedented access to information, educational resources, and learning opportunities. Online tutorials, courses, and study groups enhance their academic experiences and support self-directed learning.

- Collaborative Learning: Digital tools facilitate collaborative learning, allowing Gen Z to work on group projects, share knowledge, and engage in peer-to-peer learning regardless of geographical constraints.

2. Academic Challenges:

- Distractions and Procrastination: The allure of social media and online entertainment can lead to distractions and procrastination, affecting academic performance. Gen Z may struggle to balance screen time with study time, impacting their ability to focus on schoolwork.

- Information Overload: The vast amount of information available online can be overwhelming, making it difficult for Gen Z to filter and prioritize relevant content. This information overload can hinder their ability to concentrate and retain knowledge.

3. Professional Development:

- Digital Literacy: Gen Z's familiarity with digital tools and platforms is a significant asset in the modern workplace. Their digital literacy enables them to navigate and leverage technology effectively, enhancing their productivity and adaptability.

- Remote Work Skills: The rise of remote work aligns with Gen Z's comfort with digital communication and collaboration. They are well-equipped to thrive in virtual work environments, utilizing digital tools to stay connected and manage tasks.

Strategies for Managing Constant Connectivity

Managing the impact of constant connectivity requires conscious efforts to balance digital engagement with offline activities. Gen Z can adopt various strategies to mitigate the negative effects and enhance their well-being.

1. Digital Well-Being Practices:

- Setting Boundaries: Establishing boundaries for screen time and digital interactions can help prevent burnout and maintain a healthy balance. Techniques such as scheduling digital detoxes and setting specific times for social media use can be effective.

- Mindful Technology Use: Practicing mindfulness in technology use involves being intentional about how and when to engage with digital devices. Gen Z can benefit from being present in offline moments and avoiding mindless scrolling.

2. Building Offline Connections:

- Prioritizing Face-to-Face Interactions: Encouraging face-to-face interactions can help develop social skills and build deeper, more meaningful relationships. Engaging in activities that promote physical presence, such as sports, clubs, and social events, can enhance social well-being.

- Balancing Online and Offline Lives: Striking a balance between online and offline activities is crucial. Gen Z can benefit from pursuing hobbies and interests that do not involve screens, fostering a well-rounded lifestyle.

3. Enhancing Focus and Productivity:

    - Creating Focused Work Environments: Designing workspaces that minimize distractions can enhance focus and productivity. Using tools like focus apps, noise-canceling headphones, and dedicated study areas can help create conducive environments for deep work.

    - Time Management Techniques: Implementing time management techniques such as the Pomodoro Technique, prioritizing tasks, and setting clear goals can help Gen Z manage their time effectively and stay on track with their academic and professional responsibilities.

The impact of constant connectivity on Generation Z is multifaceted, influencing their attention spans, mental health, social interactions, and overall well-being. While the digital environment offers numerous benefits, it also presents significant challenges that require conscious management. By adopting strategies to balance digital engagement with offline activities, Gen Z can navigate the complexities of constant connectivity and leverage its advantages while mitigating its negative effects. Understanding these impacts is essential for supporting Gen Z's development and helping them thrive in a digitally connected world.

Multitasking and Attention Span

Generation Z, born approximately between 1997 and 2012, has grown up in a digitally saturated environment where multitasking is not only common but often necessary. This constant connectivity and exposure to multiple streams of information have significantly influenced their cognitive processes, particularly their attention span and ability to multitask. This chapter explores the impact of these factors on Gen Z, examining both the benefits and challenges associated with their multitasking habits and attention management.

The Nature of Multitasking

Multitasking involves engaging in more than one task simultaneously or switching rapidly between tasks. For Gen Z, multitasking is a routine part of their daily lives, facilitated by digital devices and platforms that enable seamless transitions between activities.

1. Digital Environment:

- Multiple Screens: Gen Z often uses multiple screens at once, such as smartphones, tablets, laptops, and TVs. This behavior fosters a natural tendency to multitask, as they navigate between different devices and applications.

- Diverse Activities: Typical multitasking activities include browsing social media while watching TV, texting while doing homework, or listening to music while playing video games. These combinations illustrate how Gen Z integrates various forms of entertainment, communication, and work.

2. Perceived Efficiency:

- Sense of Productivity: Many Gen Z individuals believe that multitasking enhances their productivity, allowing them to accomplish more in less time. This perception is reinforced by their ability to quickly switch between tasks and manage multiple streams of information.

- Adapting to Demands: The fast-paced nature of the digital world demands quick responses and adaptability. Gen Z's proficiency in multitasking helps them meet these demands, keeping up with rapid information flow and constant communication.

Cognitive Impact of Multitasking

While multitasking can create a sense of efficiency, it has complex effects on cognitive processes, particularly concerning attention span and task performance.

1. Attention Span:

- Fragmented Attention: Constantly switching between tasks can fragment attention, making it challenging to maintain sustained focus on a single activity. This fragmented attention can lead to superficial processing of information and reduced comprehension.

- Shortened Attention Span: The habit of frequent task switching can contribute to a shortened attention span.

Gen Z may find it difficult to engage in activities that require prolonged concentration, such as reading lengthy texts or working on complex projects without interruptions.

2. Task Performance:

- Decreased Accuracy and Efficiency: Research indicates that multitasking can decrease accuracy and efficiency. The cognitive load required to juggle multiple tasks can lead to errors and slower task completion, contradicting the perceived productivity benefits.

- Reduced Cognitive Depth: Multitasking often results in reduced cognitive depth, as the brain struggles to process and retain detailed information from multiple sources simultaneously. This can impact learning outcomes and the quality of work produced.

3. Cognitive Flexibility:

- Adaptive Thinking: Despite the challenges, multitasking can enhance cognitive flexibility, the ability to adapt thinking and behavior to new, changing, or unexpected events. Gen Z's multitasking habits may contribute to their resilience and adaptability in dynamic environments.

- Problem-Solving Skills: The practice of juggling multiple tasks can improve problem-solving skills, as Gen Z learns to prioritize, organize, and manage their time effectively.

Managing Attention in a Digital World

Given the challenges associated with multitasking, developing strategies to manage attention effectively is crucial for Gen Z's cognitive and emotional well-being.

1. Mindful Multitasking:

- Intentional Task Switching: Practicing mindful multitasking involves being intentional about when and how to switch tasks. By focusing on one task at a time and taking deliberate breaks between activities, Gen Z can enhance attention and reduce cognitive overload.

- Setting Priorities: Prioritizing tasks based on their importance and urgency can help manage multitasking more effectively. Gen Z can benefit from creating to-do lists and setting clear goals to stay organized and focused.

2. Enhancing Focus:

- Creating Distraction-Free Zones: Establishing environments that minimize distractions can support sustained focus. Designating specific areas for studying or working, free from digital interruptions, can improve concentration and task performance.

- Using Focus Techniques: Techniques such as the Pomodoro Technique, which involves working for a set period followed by a short break, can help manage attention and maintain productivity. These methods encourage regular intervals of focused work and rest.

3. Digital Well-Being:

- Managing Screen Time: Monitoring and managing screen time is essential for maintaining digital well-being. Tools and apps that track screen usage and set limits can help Gen Z balance their online and offline activities.

- Practicing Digital Detox: Taking regular digital detoxes, periods of time without digital devices, can refresh the mind and reduce the cognitive strain of constant connectivity. Engaging in offline activities such as exercise, hobbies, and face-to-face interactions can promote mental health and well-being.

4. Educational and Professional Strategies:

- Incorporating Breaks: Educators and employers can support Gen Z by incorporating regular breaks into schedules, allowing time for rest and mental recharging. Structured breaks can improve focus and productivity during work or study sessions.

- Promoting Deep Work: Encouraging deep work, periods of uninterrupted focus on a single task, can enhance cognitive depth and the quality of outcomes. Creating opportunities for deep work within educational and professional environments can support Gen Z's cognitive development.

The multitasking habits and attention span of Generation Z are significantly influenced by their digital environment. While multitasking can enhance cognitive flexibility and problem-solving skills, it also poses challenges such as fragmented attention and reduced task performance. Developing strategies to manage attention effectively, such as mindful multitasking, creating distraction-free zones, and practicing digital detox, is essential for supporting Gen Z's cognitive and emotional well-being. Understanding the impact of constant connectivity on multitasking and attention span is crucial for fostering environments that promote sustained focus, deep work, and overall mental health in this digitally native generation.

CHAPTER 05

INTERESTS AND HOBBIES

Entertainment Preferences: Gaming, Streaming, and Memes

Generation Z, born approximately between 1997 and 2012, has grown up with unprecedented access to digital entertainment. Their preferences reflect a dynamic interplay of gaming, streaming, and meme culture, all of which play a significant role in their daily lives. This chapter explores these entertainment preferences, examining their appeal, impact, and the ways in which they shape Gen Z's identity and social interactions.

Gaming

Gaming is a cornerstone of Gen Z's entertainment landscape, offering immersive experiences, social interaction, and a sense of achievement. The gaming industry has evolved significantly, providing a diverse range of options that cater to various interests and skill levels.

1. Types of Games:

- Video Games: Video games encompass a broad spectrum, from single-player narrative-driven games to massive multiplayer online (MMO) games. Popular genres include action-adventure, role-playing games (RPGs), first-person shooters (FPS), and simulation games.

- Mobile Games: The accessibility of smartphones has made mobile gaming a popular choice among Gen Z. Casual games like puzzle and strategy games, as well as more complex mobile RPGs, offer entertainment on the go.

- Esports: Competitive gaming, or esports, has gained immense popularity, with Gen Z both participating in and watching esports tournaments. Games like "League of Legends," "Fortnite," and "Valorant" are at the forefront of this trend.

2. Social Interaction in Gaming:

- Multiplayer and Online Communities: Gaming provides a platform for social interaction through multiplayer modes and online communities. Gen Z connects with friends and strangers alike, forming bonds over shared gaming experiences.

- Streaming Platforms: Platforms like Twitch and YouTube Gaming allow Gen Z to watch live streams of their favorite gamers, engage in chat discussions, and even stream their own gameplay. This interactive element enhances the social aspect of gaming.

3. Impact of Gaming:

- Cognitive Benefits: Gaming can improve cognitive skills such as problem-solving, strategic thinking, and hand-eye coordination. It also encourages perseverance and adaptability through challenging gameplay.

- Potential Downsides: Excessive gaming can lead to issues such as reduced physical activity, disrupted sleep patterns, and social isolation. Balancing gaming with other activities is crucial for maintaining overall well-being.

Streaming

Streaming services have revolutionized the way Gen Z consumes entertainment, offering on-demand access to a vast array of content. From television shows and movies to music and live events, streaming platforms cater to diverse preferences and lifestyles.

1. Video Streaming:

- Subscription Services: Platforms like Netflix, Hulu, Disney+, and Amazon Prime Video provide Gen Z with access to a wide range of TV shows, movies, and original content. The convenience of binge-watching and personalized recommendations enhance the appeal of these services.

- YouTube: YouTube remains a dominant force in Gen Z's entertainment consumption. With content ranging from vlogs and tutorials to web series and documentaries, YouTube offers something for everyone.

2. Music Streaming:

- Music Platforms: Services like Spotify, Apple Music, and SoundCloud allow Gen Z to stream their favorite music and discover new artists. Playlists, curated recommendations, and social sharing features enhance the listening experience.

- Podcasts and Audio Content: Podcasts have become increasingly popular, providing Gen Z with a diverse range of audio content, from true crime stories and educational series to comedy shows and interviews.

3. Live Streaming:

- Interactive Live Content: Platforms like Twitch, Instagram Live, and TikTok Live offer real-time interaction with content creators. Gen Z engages in live chats, Q&A sessions, and virtual events, fostering a sense of community and immediacy.

4. Impact of Streaming:

- Content Variety and Accessibility: Streaming services offer unparalleled content variety and accessibility, allowing Gen Z to explore different genres and interests easily. This diversity supports personalized entertainment experiences.

- Potential Drawbacks: The abundance of content can lead to binge-watching and screen fatigue. Managing screen time and incorporating offline activities are essential for maintaining a healthy balance.

Memes

Memes are a unique and influential form of entertainment for Gen Z, serving as a medium for humor, social commentary, and cultural expression. The rapid creation and sharing of memes reflect the dynamic nature of internet culture.

1. The Nature of Memes:

- Humor and Relatability: Memes often feature humorous and relatable content that resonates with Gen Z's experiences and sensibilities. They are shared widely across social media platforms, creating a sense of shared understanding and amusement.

- Formats and Themes: Memes come in various formats, including image macros, GIFs, and video clips. Common themes include current events, pop culture references, and everyday life scenarios.

2. Cultural Significance:

- Social Commentary: Memes can serve as a form of social commentary, addressing political issues, social justice topics, and cultural phenomena. They allow Gen Z to express opinions and engage in discussions in a lighthearted yet impactful manner.

- Viral Trends: Memes often go viral, rapidly spreading across the internet and influencing broader cultural trends. Participating in meme creation and sharing helps Gen Z stay connected with current trends and societal conversations.

3. Impact of Meme Culture:

- Community Building: Meme culture fosters a sense of community among Gen Z, as shared humor and experiences create bonds and facilitate social interaction. Online forums, meme pages, and social media groups provide spaces for collective engagement.

- Critical Thinking and Creativity: Creating and interpreting memes requires critical thinking and creativity. Gen Z develops skills in visual communication, satire, and cultural literacy through their involvement in meme culture.

Integrating Entertainment Preferences

Gen Z's entertainment preferences in gaming, streaming, and memes are not isolated; they often intersect and complement each other, creating a rich and multifaceted entertainment ecosystem.

1. Cross-Platform Engagement:

- Gaming and Streaming: Many gamers stream their gameplay on platforms like Twitch and YouTube, combining their love for gaming with the interactive nature of streaming. This integration enhances the entertainment experience and builds communities around shared interests.

- Memes and Streaming Content: Popular shows, movies, and music often inspire meme creation, blending streaming content with meme culture. This interplay allows Gen Z to engage with their favorite media in creative and humorous ways.

2. Community and Social Interaction:

- Shared Experiences: Gaming, streaming, and meme culture provide common ground for social interaction. Gen Z connects with peers through these shared experiences, building friendships and communities around their entertainment preferences.

- Digital Identity: These entertainment preferences also contribute to the formation of digital identity. Gen Z expresses their interests, values, and humor through the content they consume, create, and share.

Generation Z's entertainment preferences reflect a dynamic blend of gaming, streaming, and meme culture. These activities provide immersive experiences, social interaction, and avenues for self-expression, shaping their daily lives and identities. While these forms of entertainment offer numerous benefits, such as cognitive development, creativity, and community building, they also present challenges that require mindful management. Understanding Gen Z's entertainment preferences is essential for appreciating their unique perspectives and the ways in which they navigate the digital world. By balancing these activities with offline engagement and fostering healthy habits, Gen Z can continue to enjoy the rich and diverse landscape of digital entertainment.

Educational Pursuits: Online Learning and DIY Culture

Generation Z, born approximately between 1997 and 2012, is often characterized by their proactive approach to learning and self-improvement. This chapter delves into Gen Z's educational pursuits, with a particular focus on online learning and the do-it-yourself (DIY) culture. These educational preferences reflect their adaptability, resourcefulness, and desire for personalized, flexible learning experiences.

Online Learning

Online learning has become a significant aspect of education for Gen Z, offering accessibility, flexibility, and a wealth of resources that cater to their diverse interests and needs.

1. Access to Information:

- E-Learning Platforms: Platforms such as Coursera, edX, Udemy, and Khan Academy provide access to a vast array of courses on virtually any topic. These platforms partner with universities and institutions worldwide, allowing Gen Z to learn from top educators without geographical constraints.

- YouTube and Educational Channels: YouTube is a treasure trove of educational content, with channels dedicated to subjects ranging from science and math to history and art. Content creators like CrashCourse, Khan Academy, and TED-Ed have made complex topics accessible and engaging.

2. Flexibility and Convenience:

- Self-Paced Learning: Online learning allows Gen Z to learn at their own pace, fitting education into their schedules as needed. This flexibility is particularly beneficial for balancing school, work, and personal commitments.

- Anytime, Anywhere: The ability to access educational materials from anywhere with an internet connection makes learning more accessible. Gen Z can study from home, in transit, or during breaks, maximizing their use of time.

3. Diverse Learning Styles:

- Multimedia and Interactive Content: Online courses often incorporate multimedia elements such as videos, animations, and interactive quizzes, catering to Gen Z's preference for engaging, visual content. These formats help maintain interest and enhance comprehension.

- Personalized Learning Paths: Adaptive learning technologies personalize the educational experience, tailoring content and recommendations based on individual progress and preferences. This personalized approach helps address specific learning needs and goals.

4. Collaborative Learning:

- Virtual Study Groups: Online platforms facilitate collaborative learning through virtual study groups and forums. Gen Z can connect with peers worldwide, share insights, and work on projects together, fostering a sense of community and support.

- Instructor Interaction: Many online courses offer opportunities for direct interaction with instructors through live sessions, discussion boards, and office hours. This access to expert guidance enhances the learning experience.

5. Certification and Career Advancement:

- Professional Development: Online learning provides opportunities for professional development, with courses and certifications that can enhance resumes and career prospects. Gen Z can acquire new skills or improve existing ones to stay competitive in the job market.

- Specialized Knowledge: From coding bootcamps to advanced degrees, online education allows Gen Z to pursue specialized knowledge in their fields of interest, often at a lower cost and with greater flexibility than traditional education.

DIY Culture

The DIY (do-it-yourself) culture is another hallmark of Gen Z's educational pursuits, reflecting their inclination towards hands-on, practical learning and creativity.

1. Empowerment and Independence:

- Self-Reliance: DIY culture fosters a sense of self-reliance and empowerment. Gen Z takes pride in learning new skills and completing projects independently, whether it's fixing a bike, building furniture, or crafting handmade gifts.

- Resourcefulness: The DIY approach encourages resourcefulness, as individuals seek out materials, tools, and information to accomplish their goals. This mindset helps Gen Z develop problem-solving skills and adaptability.

2. Creative Expression:

- Personal Projects: DIY projects provide an outlet for creative expression. Gen Z engages in activities like art, fashion, home decor, and upcycling, using their skills to create personalized, unique items.

- Online Inspiration and Tutorials: Platforms like Pinterest, Instagram, and YouTube are rich sources of DIY inspiration and tutorials. Gen Z can find step-by-step guides and creative ideas to spark their imagination and guide their projects.

3. Sustainable Living:

- Eco-Friendly Practices: The DIY culture aligns with Gen Z's commitment to sustainability. They often engage in practices such as recycling, repurposing materials, and making eco-friendly products, contributing to environmental conservation.

- Minimalism and Self-Sufficiency: DIY projects promote minimalism and self-sufficiency, encouraging Gen Z to make rather than buy, reduce waste, and lead more sustainable lifestyles.

4. Community and Collaboration:

- Maker Communities: Online and offline maker communities provide support and collaboration opportunities for DIY enthusiasts. Gen Z can share their projects, seek advice, and collaborate on initiatives within these communities.

- Workshops and Events: DIY workshops and events offer hands-on learning experiences and social interaction. Gen Z participates in local craft fairs, maker fairs, and skill-sharing events to learn new techniques and connect with like-minded individuals.

5. Skill Development:

- Practical Skills: DIY projects help Gen Z develop practical skills that are valuable in everyday life. From basic carpentry and sewing to digital skills like graphic design and coding, these competencies enhance their self-sufficiency and creativity.

- Innovation and Experimentation: The DIY mindset encourages innovation and experimentation. Gen Z learns to think outside the box, try new methods, and embrace trial and error, fostering a growth mindset and resilience.

Integrating Online Learning and DIY Culture

Gen Z's online learning and DIY culture often intersect, creating a rich, multifaceted approach to education and self-improvement.

1. Blended Learning Experiences:

- Combining Theory and Practice: Online courses provide theoretical knowledge, while DIY projects offer practical application. Gen Z blends these experiences to deepen their understanding and skill set. For example, they might take an online coding course and then create their own website or app.

- Interactive Learning Platforms: Platforms like Skillshare and Instructables offer courses that integrate DIY projects, allowing Gen Z to learn by doing. These platforms provide structured lessons and community support, bridging the gap between online learning and hands-on practice.

2. Building Digital and Physical Skills:

- Tech-Enhanced DIY: Digital tools and technologies enhance DIY projects, from 3D printing and digital design to electronics and robotics. Gen Z leverages online resources to learn these skills and apply them to innovative DIY creations.

- Hybrid Workshops: Virtual and in-person workshops offer hybrid learning experiences. Gen Z can participate in online classes with live demonstrations, followed by hands-on practice at home or in community maker spaces.

3. Collaborative Learning and Sharing:

- Online Communities: Online communities facilitate the sharing of knowledge and projects. Gen Z collaborates with peers, mentors, and experts, gaining insights and feedback that enrich their learning journey.

- Social Media Integration: Social media platforms enable Gen Z to document and share their DIY projects and learning experiences. This sharing fosters a culture of continuous learning and mutual inspiration.

Generation Z's educational pursuits are characterized by a blend of online learning and DIY culture. These approaches reflect their desire for flexible, personalized, and practical education that empowers them to develop new skills, express creativity, and lead sustainable lives. By integrating online learning with hands-on projects, Gen Z creates a rich and multifaceted educational experience that supports their growth and adaptability in an ever-changing world. Understanding and supporting these educational preferences is essential for fostering Gen Z's potential and preparing them for future challenges and opportunities.

Social Activities: Virtual Hangouts and Digital Communities

Generation Z, born approximately between 1997 and 2012, has grown up in a world where social interactions are increasingly mediated by digital technology. As digital natives, they have developed unique ways of connecting and building relationships through virtual hangouts and digital communities. This chapter explores the nature of these social activities, examining their appeal, impact, and the ways in which they shape Gen Z's social lives and identities.

Virtual Hangouts

Virtual hangouts have become a staple in the social lives of Gen Z, offering a convenient and versatile way to connect with friends and family. These online gatherings can take various forms, from casual video chats to more structured online events.

1. Video Chat Platforms:

- Zoom, Skype, and Google Meet: These platforms, initially popularized for professional and educational use, have also become key tools for socializing. Gen Z uses them for group video calls, virtual parties, and study sessions.

- Facetime and WhatsApp: For more personal and informal interactions, Gen Z often relies on mobile video chat apps like FaceTime and WhatsApp. These platforms allow for spontaneous and intimate conversations.

2. Virtual Events and Parties:

- Online Gaming Parties: Multiplayer games such as "Fortnite," "Among Us," and "Minecraft" serve as virtual hangout spaces where Gen Z can play and socialize simultaneously. These gaming sessions often include voice or video chat, enhancing the social experience.

- Virtual Watch Parties: Platforms like Netflix Party and Disney+ GroupWatch enable synchronized viewing of movies and TV shows, allowing friends to watch together and chat in real-time, replicating the experience of a movie night.

3. Social Media Live Sessions:

- Instagram Live and Facebook Live: Social media platforms offer live streaming features where Gen Z can host live sessions, engage with viewers in real-time, and foster interactive discussions. These sessions can range from casual hangouts to Q&A sessions and virtual concerts.

4. Impact of Virtual Hangouts:

- Maintaining Connections: Virtual hangouts help Gen Z maintain relationships across distances, providing a sense of closeness and continuity in friendships and family bonds.

- Inclusivity and Accessibility: These platforms make socializing more inclusive and accessible, especially for individuals with mobility issues or those living in remote areas.

Digital Communities

Digital communities are another vital aspect of Gen Z's social landscape, providing spaces for like-minded individuals to connect, share interests, and support each other.

1. Online Forums and Groups:

- Reddit and Discord: Platforms like Reddit and Discord host numerous communities focused on specific topics, hobbies, or interests. These spaces allow Gen Z to engage in discussions, share content, and collaborate on projects.

- Facebook Groups: Facebook Groups cater to a wide range of interests, from niche hobbies to professional networks. Gen Z participates in these groups to seek advice, share experiences, and build connections.

2. Niche Social Networks:

- Interest-Based Platforms: Platforms like Wattpad for writers, ArtStation for artists, and GitHub for developers provide dedicated spaces for creative and professional communities. Gen Z uses these platforms to showcase their work, receive feedback, and connect with peers.

- Fan Communities: Fan communities centered around music, TV shows, movies, and books thrive on platforms like Tumblr, Twitter, and dedicated fan forums. These spaces allow Gen Z to express their fandom, create fan content, and engage with fellow fans.

3. Impact of Digital Communities:

- Sense of Belonging: Digital communities provide a sense of belonging and identity, helping Gen Z find their tribe and feel connected to others who share their passions and values.

- Support and Solidarity: These communities offer support and solidarity, particularly for marginalized groups. Gen Z can find safe spaces to discuss issues, seek advice, and receive emotional support.

The Intersection of Virtual Hangouts and Digital Communities

Virtual hangouts and digital communities often intersect, creating rich, multifaceted social experiences for Gen Z.

1. Hybrid Social Activities:

- Virtual Events in Digital Communities: Online communities frequently organize virtual events, such as webinars, workshops, and game nights. These events combine the social aspect of hangouts with the shared interests of digital communities, fostering deeper connections.

- Collaborative Projects: Digital communities often engage in collaborative projects, such as creating digital art, developing open-source software, or organizing social campaigns. Virtual hangouts facilitate real-time collaboration and brainstorming sessions.

2. Content Creation and Sharing:

- Live Streams and Webinars: Gen Z participates in and hosts live streams and webinars on platforms like Twitch, YouTube, and Instagram. These sessions allow them to share knowledge, entertain, and engage with their audience in real-time.

- Interactive Content: Interactive content such as live polls, Q&A sessions, and collaborative storytelling enhances the engagement and dynamism of virtual hangouts and digital communities.

Challenges and Opportunities

While virtual hangouts and digital communities offer numerous benefits, they also present challenges that need to be addressed to ensure healthy and meaningful social interactions.

1. Challenges:

- Screen Fatigue: Prolonged use of digital devices for socializing can lead to screen fatigue, causing physical discomfort and mental exhaustion. It is essential to balance online and offline activities to maintain well-being.

- Privacy and Security: The digital nature of these interactions raises concerns about privacy and security. Gen Z must navigate issues such as data protection, cyberbullying, and online harassment to create safe online environments.

2. Opportunities:

- Global Connectivity: Virtual hangouts and digital communities break down geographical barriers, allowing Gen Z to connect with people from different cultures and backgrounds. This global connectivity fosters cross-cultural understanding and broadens their perspectives.

- Empowerment through Technology: The ability to organize, collaborate, and create through digital platforms empowers Gen Z to take initiative, lead projects, and make an impact. These skills are valuable for personal development and future career opportunities.

Strategies for Enhancing Digital Social Interactions

To maximize the benefits and minimize the drawbacks of virtual hangouts and digital communities, Gen Z can adopt several strategies.

1. Balancing Online and Offline Interactions:

- Scheduled Breaks: Incorporating scheduled breaks from screens and engaging in offline activities can help mitigate screen fatigue and promote a healthy balance.

- Offline Meetups: Whenever possible, transitioning online connections to offline meetups can strengthen relationships and provide a different dynamic to social interactions.

2. Creating Safe and Inclusive Spaces:

- Moderation and Guidelines: Implementing moderation and clear guidelines in digital communities can help prevent harassment and ensure respectful interactions.

- Privacy Settings: Utilizing privacy settings and being mindful of sharing personal information can enhance security and protect against online threats.

3. Encouraging Meaningful Engagement:

- Quality over Quantity: Focusing on the quality of interactions rather than the quantity can lead to more meaningful and fulfilling social experiences.

- Active Participation: Encouraging active participation, such as contributing to discussions, sharing content, and supporting others, can enhance the sense of community and belonging.

Virtual hangouts and digital communities play a pivotal role in the social lives of Generation Z, offering platforms for connection, collaboration, and self-expression. These digital spaces provide opportunities for maintaining relationships, finding support, and engaging with diverse interests and communities. By adopting strategies to balance online and offline interactions, ensure privacy and security, and foster meaningful engagement, Gen Z can navigate the complexities of digital socializing effectively. Understanding the dynamics of virtual hangouts and digital communities is essential for appreciating the unique ways in which Gen Z builds and maintains social connections in a digitally connected world.

CHAPTER 06

SOCIAL INTERACTIONS AND RELATIONSHIP

Communication Styles

Generation Z, born approximately between 1997 and 2012, has grown up in an era of rapid technological advancements and pervasive digital connectivity. This unique environment has significantly influenced their communication styles, shaping how they interact, express themselves, and build relationships. This chapter explores the distinct communication styles of Gen Z, examining the impact of digital media, the nuances of online and offline communication, and the implications for their social interactions and relationships.

Digital-First Communication

For Gen Z, digital communication is the norm. They are more likely to reach for their smartphones to send a text or post on social media than to make a phone call or meet in person. This digital-first approach has several key characteristics.

1. Text-Based Communication:

- Instant Messaging: Platforms like WhatsApp, Messenger, and Snapchat are primary tools for daily communication. Gen Z prefers the immediacy and convenience of instant messaging over traditional phone calls or emails.

- Social Media: Social media platforms such as Instagram, Twitter, and TikTok are integral to how Gen Z communicates. They use these platforms to share updates, engage with content, and connect with friends and followers.

2. Visual and Multimedia Communication:

- Emojis and GIFs: Gen Z frequently uses emojis, GIFs, and stickers to enhance their text-based communication. These visual elements add emotion, humor, and nuance, making messages more expressive and engaging.

- Video Content: Video communication is also prevalent. Platforms like Snapchat and TikTok allow users to create and share short video clips, while video calling apps like FaceTime and Zoom facilitate real-time visual interactions.

3. Abbreviations and Slang:

- Concise Language: Gen Z often uses abbreviations, acronyms, and internet slang to communicate more efficiently. Phrases like "LOL" (laugh out loud), "BRB" (be right back), and "FOMO" (fear of missing out) are commonplace.

- Evolving Lexicon: The lexicon of Gen Z is dynamic and constantly evolving, influenced by internet culture, memes, and trends. This evolving language reflects their creativity and adaptability in digital communication.

Online vs. Offline Communication

The distinction between online and offline communication is significant for Gen Z, as each mode has its own set of norms, benefits, and challenges.

1. Online Communication:

- Anonymity and Confidence: The relative anonymity of online communication can boost confidence, allowing Gen Z to express themselves more freely and explore different aspects of their identity.

- Accessibility and Convenience: Online communication is accessible and convenient, enabling Gen Z to stay connected with friends and family regardless of geographical distances.

- Potential for Miscommunication: However, the lack of non-verbal cues in text-based communication can lead to misunderstandings. Tone and intent can be difficult to convey accurately, resulting in potential miscommunication.

2. Offline Communication:

- Face-to-Face Interaction: Offline communication, particularly face-to-face interaction, provides richer, more nuanced exchanges. Non-verbal cues such as body language, facial expressions, and tone of voice play a crucial role in conveying meaning and emotion.

- Building Deeper Connections: In-person interactions often lead to deeper, more meaningful connections. They foster empathy, understanding, and trust, which are essential for building strong relationships.

- Challenges of In-Person Communication: Some members of Gen Z may find offline communication challenging, especially if they are more accustomed to digital interactions. Developing strong interpersonal skills is crucial for navigating face-to-face communication effectively.

The Role of Social Media

Social media platforms are central to Gen Z's communication style, shaping how they share information, build relationships, and express themselves.

1. Public and Private Sharing:

- Public Posts: Platforms like Instagram and Twitter allow Gen Z to share aspects of their lives publicly, curating their online persona and engaging with a broad audience. Public posts can foster a sense of community and belonging.

- Private Messaging: Private messaging features on social media enable more intimate, one-on-one conversations. Apps like Instagram Direct and Snapchat provide spaces for private, real-time interactions.

2. Influencer Culture:

- Connecting with Influencers: Gen Z often interacts with influencers and content creators, seeing them as relatable figures who share their interests and values. This interaction can shape their opinions, tastes, and behaviors.

- Becoming Influencers: Many Gen Z individuals aspire to become influencers themselves, using social media platforms to build their brand, share their passions, and connect with followers.

3. Impact on Self-Expression:

- Creative Expression: Social media offers a platform for creative expression, allowing Gen Z to showcase their talents, share their thoughts, and create content that reflects their identity.

- Social Validation: The pursuit of likes, comments, and shares can impact self-esteem and social validation. While positive feedback can boost confidence, negative interactions or lack of engagement can lead to stress and anxiety.

Digital Etiquette and Norms

The digital communication landscape has its own set of etiquette and norms that Gen Z navigates adeptly.

1. Communication Speed:

- Expectation of Immediate Responses: There is an expectation for quick responses in digital communication. Delayed replies can be perceived as a lack of interest or engagement, leading to potential misunderstandings.

- Balancing Responsiveness and Boundaries: Managing this expectation while maintaining personal boundaries is essential. Gen Z often navigates this balance by setting clear expectations and using tools like "Do Not Disturb" modes.

2. Privacy and Transparency:

- Privacy Concerns: Gen Z is increasingly aware of privacy issues and the importance of protecting personal information online. They use privacy settings to control who can see their content and are cautious about sharing sensitive information.

- Authenticity and Transparency: Authenticity is highly valued in digital communication. Gen Z appreciates transparency and honesty, both in their interactions with peers and in the content they consume from influencers and brands.

3. Respect and Inclusivity:

- Respectful Communication: Digital etiquette emphasizes respectful and considerate communication. Gen Z is conscious of the impact of their words and strives to engage in positive, supportive interactions.

- Inclusivity and Representation: Inclusivity is a core value for Gen Z. They advocate for diverse representation and inclusivity in digital spaces, ensuring that all voices are heard and respected.

Implications for Relationships

The communication styles of Gen Z have significant implications for their relationships, both personal and professional.

1. Personal Relationships:

- Maintaining Long-Distance Friendships: Digital communication enables Gen Z to maintain long-distance friendships and relationships, providing a sense of continuity and connection despite physical separation.

- Navigating Romantic Relationships: Online dating apps and social media play a role in how Gen Z navigates romantic relationships. They use these platforms to meet potential partners, communicate, and express affection.

2. Professional Relationships:

- Networking and Career Building: Gen Z leverages digital platforms like LinkedIn for networking and career building. Their proficiency in digital communication helps them establish professional connections and pursue opportunities.

- Remote Work and Collaboration: The rise of remote work aligns with Gen Z's digital-first communication style. They are adept at using digital tools for remote collaboration, project management, and communication with colleagues.

Generation Z's communication styles are shaped by their digital upbringing, characterized by text-based messaging, visual and multimedia content, and a dynamic lexicon of abbreviations and slang. The interplay between online and offline communication, the central role of social media, and the adherence to digital etiquette and norms define how they interact and build relationships. Understanding these communication styles is essential for appreciating the unique ways in which Gen Z navigates their social interactions and relationships in a digitally connected world. By balancing digital and face-to-face communication, respecting privacy and inclusivity, and fostering meaningful connections, Gen Z can thrive in both their personal and professional lives.

Online vs. Offline Friendships

Generation Z, born approximately between 1997 and 2012, has experienced a unique blend of online and offline interactions throughout their formative years. This chapter explores the dynamics of online versus offline friendships, highlighting the benefits and challenges of each, and examining how Gen Z navigates these different modes of social connection.

Online Friendships

Online friendships have become increasingly common among Gen Z, facilitated by social media platforms, gaming communities, and other digital spaces. These friendships often provide a sense of connection and support that transcends geographical boundaries.

1. Formation and Development:

- Social Media and Forums: Platforms like Instagram, Twitter, Reddit, and TikTok allow users to connect over shared interests, hobbies, and causes. Gen Z frequently forms friendships through interactions on these platforms, where common ground fosters initial connections.

- Gaming Communities: Online multiplayer games like "Fortnite," "Minecraft," and "League of Legends" create environments where players can interact, collaborate, and form bonds. These gaming communities often serve as a foundation for lasting friendships.

2. Characteristics of Online Friendships:

- Diverse Networks: Online friendships often involve diverse networks, including people from different cultural, geographical, and socioeconomic backgrounds. This diversity enriches the social experience and broadens perspectives.

- Anonymity and Confidence: The relative anonymity of online interactions can boost confidence, allowing individuals to express themselves more freely and explore different facets of their identity without fear of judgment.

3. Communication Styles:

- Text-Based and Visual Communication: Online friendships primarily rely on text-based communication through messaging apps, forums, and social media comments. Emojis, GIFs, and memes enhance these interactions, adding emotional nuance and humor.

- Video and Voice Calls: Platforms like Discord, Zoom, and FaceTime facilitate more personal interactions through video and voice calls. These tools help maintain the human element in online friendships, making interactions more engaging and intimate.

4. Benefits of Online Friendships:

- Accessibility and Convenience: Online friendships offer accessibility and convenience, allowing Gen Z to maintain connections regardless of physical distance. This is particularly valuable for those with mobility issues or living in remote areas.

- Supportive Communities: Online spaces often provide supportive communities where individuals can share experiences, seek advice, and find emotional support. These communities can be especially beneficial for marginalized groups.

5. Challenges of Online Friendships:

- Lack of Physical Presence: The absence of physical presence can limit the depth of connection in online friendships. Non-verbal cues like body language and facial expressions, which are crucial for building empathy and understanding, are often missing.

- Potential for Miscommunication: Text-based communication can sometimes lead to misunderstandings, as tone and intent are harder to convey accurately. This can result in conflicts or feelings of disconnect.

Offline Friendships

Offline friendships, formed through face-to-face interactions, continue to play a significant role in the social lives of Gen Z. These friendships provide opportunities for deeper connections and shared experiences that are unique to in-person interactions.

1. Formation and Development:

- School and Extracurricular Activities: Many offline friendships begin in school settings or through participation in extracurricular activities such as sports teams, clubs, and volunteer organizations. These environments facilitate regular, structured interactions that help build trust and familiarity.

- Community and Social Events: Community events, social gatherings, and family connections also contribute to the formation of offline friendships. These settings offer opportunities for spontaneous interactions and shared experiences.

2. Characteristics of Offline Friendships:

- Physical Presence: The physical presence in offline friendships allows for the exchange of non-verbal cues, such as body language, facial expressions, and touch. These cues enhance communication and help build deeper emotional connections.

- Shared Activities: Offline friendships often involve shared activities and experiences, such as studying together, playing sports, or attending events. These shared moments create memories and strengthen bonds.

3. Communication Styles:

- Face-to-Face Interaction: Face-to-face communication provides richer, more nuanced exchanges, fostering empathy and understanding. Gen Z values the immediacy and authenticity of in-person interactions.

- Complementary Digital Communication: Even in offline friendships, digital communication tools like texting and social media play a complementary role. These tools help maintain connections between face-to-face meetings and facilitate coordination of plans.

4. Benefits of Offline Friendships:

- Deeper Connections: The depth of connection in offline friendships is often enhanced by physical presence and shared experiences. These friendships provide a sense of stability and support that is rooted in real-world interactions.

- Holistic Development: Engaging in face-to-face interactions helps develop social skills such as active listening, conflict resolution, and emotional intelligence. These skills are crucial for personal and professional growth.

5. Challenges of Offline Friendships:

- Geographical Limitations: Offline friendships are often limited by geographical proximity, making it challenging to maintain connections when friends move away or have conflicting schedules.

- Time and Effort: Maintaining offline friendships requires time and effort, including regular meet-ups and participation in shared activities. Balancing these commitments with other responsibilities can be challenging.

Balancing Online and Offline Friendships

For Gen Z, balancing online and offline friendships is key to maintaining a well-rounded social life. Each type of friendship offers unique benefits and challenges, and integrating both can enhance overall social well-being.

1. Hybrid Social Activities:

- Combining Online and Offline Interactions: Gen Z often combines online and offline interactions to strengthen friendships. For example, they might play online games with friends during the week and meet up in person on weekends.

- Virtual Events with Real-World Elements: Virtual events that incorporate real-world elements, such as watching a movie together online while chatting via video call, blend the convenience of online interactions with the shared experience of offline activities.

2. Maintaining Balance:

- Setting Boundaries: Setting boundaries for screen time and offline activities helps maintain a healthy balance. Gen Z can schedule specific times for digital interactions and prioritize face-to-face meet-ups to nurture both types of friendships.

- Mindful Engagement: Being mindful of the quality of interactions, rather than just the quantity, can enhance the depth and satisfaction of both online and offline friendships. Focusing on meaningful conversations and shared experiences is key.

3. Leveraging Technology:

- Facilitating Offline Connections: Technology can facilitate offline connections by helping Gen Z coordinate plans, share updates, and stay in touch between meet-ups. Apps like Google Calendar, Doodle, and event planning tools can streamline this process.

- Supporting Long-Distance Friendships: For long-distance friendships, technology provides a lifeline that keeps connections strong. Regular video calls, social media interactions, and virtual hangouts help bridge the gap created by physical distance.

Implications for Social Development

The interplay between online and offline friendships has significant implications for the social development of Gen Z.

1. Adaptability and Resilience:

- Navigating Different Contexts: The ability to navigate different social contexts, both online and offline, fosters adaptability and resilience. Gen Z learns to adjust their communication styles and social strategies based on the medium of interaction.

- Building Diverse Skills: Engaging in both online and offline friendships helps develop a diverse set of social skills. These include digital literacy, online etiquette, empathy, and in-person communication competencies.

2. Enhanced Social Networks:

- Broader Social Circles: The combination of online and offline friendships expands social circles, providing access to a wider range of perspectives, support networks, and opportunities.

- Inclusive Social Practices: The inclusivity of online spaces allows Gen Z to connect with individuals who share similar interests and experiences, while offline interactions reinforce local community ties and personal connections.

Generation Z's social interactions are characterized by a dynamic blend of online and offline friendships. Each mode of interaction offers unique benefits and challenges, contributing to the richness and complexity of their social lives. By balancing digital and face-to-face interactions, setting boundaries, and leveraging technology, Gen Z can nurture meaningful relationships that support their social and emotional well-being. Understanding the interplay between online and offline friendships is essential for appreciating the diverse ways in which Gen Z connects, communicates, and builds relationships in a digitally connected world.

Dating and Romance in the Digital Age

Generation Z, born approximately between 1997 and 2012, is navigating dating and romance in a world where digital technology plays a central role. This chapter explores how Gen Z approaches dating and relationships in the digital age, examining the impact of dating apps, social media, and other online platforms on their romantic interactions. We will also discuss the benefits and challenges of digital dating and the implications for emotional and relational well-being.

The Role of Technology in Dating

For Gen Z, technology is deeply integrated into their dating lives, shaping how they meet potential partners, communicate, and maintain relationships.

1. Dating Apps and Websites:

- Popular Platforms: Dating apps like Tinder, Bumble, and Hinge are widely used by Gen Z to meet new people. These platforms offer a convenient way to connect with potential partners based on location, interests, and preferences.

- Niche Dating Apps: There are also niche dating apps catering to specific interests or communities, such as JSwipe for Jewish singles or HER for LGBTQ+ women, allowing Gen Z to find partners with shared values or backgrounds.

2. Social Media and Online Presence:

- Profile Curation: Social media profiles on Instagram, Snapchat, and TikTok often serve as extensions of dating profiles. Gen Z carefully curates their online presence to attract potential partners and showcase their interests and personality.

- Direct Messaging: Social media platforms also provide a space for direct messaging, enabling Gen Z to flirt, get to know each other, and maintain ongoing communication.

3. Virtual Communication:

- Video Calls and Virtual Dates: Video calling platforms like Zoom, FaceTime, and Google Meet facilitate virtual dates, especially during times when meeting in person may be challenging. These virtual interactions help maintain intimacy and connection.

- Texting and Instant Messaging: Texting and instant messaging remain primary modes of communication, allowing for continuous contact and real-time conversations.

Benefits of Digital Dating

Digital dating offers several advantages that appeal to Gen Z, making it an attractive option for building romantic relationships.

1. Convenience and Accessibility:

- Ease of Meeting New People: Dating apps and social media make it easier for Gen Z to meet new people beyond their immediate social circles. This expands their opportunities for finding compatible partners.

- Flexible Communication: Digital communication allows for flexibility in terms of time and location. Gen Z can chat and connect with potential partners at their convenience, without the need for physical presence.

2. Enhanced Compatibility Matching:

- Algorithmic Matching: Many dating apps use algorithms to match users based on compatibility factors such as interests, values, and personality traits. This increases the likelihood of finding a good match.

- Filtering Options: Dating platforms often provide filtering options to narrow down potential matches based on specific criteria, helping Gen Z focus on partners who meet their preferences.

3. Safety and Comfort:

- Control Over Interaction: Digital dating allows for a level of control over interactions. Gen Z can choose to engage or disengage with potential partners without the pressure of in-person encounters.

- Comfort in Initial Interactions: For those who may feel shy or anxious about face-to-face interactions, digital dating offers a more comfortable and less intimidating way to initiate conversations and build connections.

Challenges of Digital Dating

Despite its benefits, digital dating also presents several challenges that Gen Z must navigate to build healthy and meaningful relationships.

1. Superficial Interactions:

- Emphasis on Appearance: The visual nature of dating apps and social media can lead to an emphasis on appearance, potentially overshadowing other important aspects of compatibility. This can result in superficial judgments and interactions.

- Brief Engagements: The ease of swiping and moving on to the next profile can lead to brief and shallow engagements, making it challenging to develop deeper connections.

2. Miscommunication and Misrepresentation:

- Lack of Non-Verbal Cues: Text-based communication lacks non-verbal cues such as tone, facial expressions, and body language, which are crucial for understanding context and intent. This can lead to misunderstandings and miscommunication.

- Catfishing and Deception: The anonymity of digital interactions can sometimes result in deception, where individuals misrepresent themselves or engage in catfishing, posing as someone they are not.

3. Emotional Impact:

- Ghosting and Rejection: The prevalence of ghosting (suddenly cutting off all communication without explanation) and frequent rejection can take an emotional toll, leading to feelings of insecurity and frustration.

- Pressure to Maintain Online Persona: The need to maintain a carefully curated online persona can create pressure and anxiety, affecting self-esteem and authenticity in relationships.

Navigating Digital Dating

To navigate the complexities of digital dating effectively, Gen Z can adopt several strategies to foster healthy and meaningful romantic relationships.

1. Authenticity and Honesty:

- Being Genuine: Emphasizing authenticity and being genuine in online interactions can help build trust and attract like-minded individuals. Presenting oneself honestly and openly sets the foundation for meaningful connections.

- Setting Clear Intentions: Communicating intentions clearly, whether seeking a casual fling or a serious relationship, helps manage expectations and reduces misunderstandings.

2. Balancing Online and Offline Interactions:

- Transitioning to Offline Dates: Moving from online to offline interactions is crucial for developing deeper connections. Gen Z should prioritize meeting in person once a level of comfort and trust has been established online.

- Maintaining Digital Boundaries: Setting boundaries for digital communication, such as designated times for texting or video calls, helps balance online and offline life and prevents burnout.

3. Prioritizing Emotional Well-Being:

- Managing Rejection and Ghosting: Developing resilience to rejection and ghosting is essential for emotional well-being. Gen Z can benefit from understanding that these experiences are common in digital dating and not a reflection of their worth.

- Seeking Support: Turning to friends, family, or professional counselors for support and advice can provide valuable perspective and help navigate the emotional ups and downs of digital dating.

4. Staying Safe Online:

- Protecting Personal Information: Being cautious about sharing personal information and using privacy settings on dating apps and social media can enhance safety. Gen Z should avoid disclosing sensitive details until they feel secure in the relationship.

- Meeting in Safe Locations: For in-person dates, choosing public and safe locations for initial meetings is important. Letting a trusted friend or family member know about the date plans can provide an additional layer of safety.

Implications for Long-Term Relationships

The way Gen Z navigates dating in the digital age has implications for the development of long-term relationships and partnerships.

1. Building Trust and Intimacy:

- Gradual Development: Trust and intimacy in digital dating often develop gradually. Gen Z should focus on consistent communication, shared experiences, and mutual respect to build strong foundations for long-term relationships.

- Emotional Availability: Being emotionally available and open to vulnerability is crucial for deepening connections and fostering intimacy. Gen Z should prioritize emotional honesty and support within their relationships.

2. Navigating Relationship Milestones:

- Defining the Relationship: Clear communication about relationship status and goals helps navigate milestones such as exclusivity, meeting each other's families, and future plans. Gen Z should ensure that both partners are aligned in their expectations.

- Managing Digital Presence: As relationships progress, managing digital presence and social media interactions becomes important. Gen Z should establish boundaries around online behavior, such as sharing relationship details and interacting with others.

3. Adapting to Changes and Challenges:

- Flexibility and Adaptability: Long-term relationships require flexibility and adaptability to navigate changes and challenges. Gen Z should develop problem-solving skills and a willingness to compromise to sustain their partnerships.

- Continual Growth and Support: Supporting each other's personal growth and maintaining a sense of individuality within the relationship are essential for long-term success. Gen Z should encourage and celebrate each other's achievements and growth.

Dating and romance in the digital age present unique opportunities and challenges for Generation Z. The integration of technology into their romantic lives has transformed how they meet, communicate, and build relationships. By navigating digital dating with authenticity, balancing online and offline interactions, prioritizing emotional well-being, and staying safe, Gen Z can foster meaningful and fulfilling romantic connections. Understanding the dynamics of digital dating is essential for appreciating the ways in which Gen Z experiences love and relationships in a digitally connected world.

CHAPTER 07

THE BUYING DECISIONS OF GEN Z

Purchasing Power and Economic Impact

Generation Z, born approximately between 1997 and 2012, is emerging as a significant economic force. With unique preferences, values, and behaviors, their buying decisions are reshaping markets and influencing the economy in profound ways. This chapter explores the purchasing power of Gen Z, examining their economic impact, the factors driving their buying decisions, and the implications for businesses and the broader economy.

The Purchasing Power of Gen Z

Gen Z's purchasing power is substantial and growing, driven by their increasing influence as consumers and their entry into the workforce.

1. Early Economic Participation:

- Part-Time Jobs and Gigs: Many Gen Z individuals start working early, often taking on part-time jobs, freelance gigs, or side hustles while still in school. This early economic participation provides them with disposable income and shapes their financial habits.

- Entrepreneurial Spirit: Gen Z is known for its entrepreneurial spirit, with many young individuals starting their own businesses or monetizing their skills through platforms like Etsy, YouTube, and social media. This entrepreneurial activity contributes to their economic independence and purchasing power.

2. Influence on Household Spending:

- Family Purchases: Even before earning their own income, Gen Z has a significant influence on household spending. Their preferences and opinions often shape family decisions on products such as technology, fashion, and entertainment.

- Peer Influence: Gen Z's buying decisions are heavily influenced by their peers, both online and offline. Social media trends, influencer endorsements, and peer recommendations play a crucial role in their purchasing choices.

3. Economic Independence:

- Entry into the Workforce: As Gen Z enters the workforce full-time, their purchasing power is set to increase dramatically. Their financial independence enables them to make substantial economic contributions and invest in a wide range of products and services.

- Financial Savvy: Growing up during economic uncertainty, many Gen Z individuals are financially savvy and cautious with their spending. They prioritize value for money and are mindful of their financial future, influencing their spending patterns.

Factors Driving Gen Z's Buying Decisions

Several key factors drive the buying decisions of Gen Z, reflecting their values, preferences, and digital upbringing.

1. Values-Driven Consumption:

- Sustainability and Ethics: Gen Z places a high value on sustainability and ethical practices. They prefer brands that demonstrate environmental responsibility, social justice, and ethical sourcing. Companies that align with these values are more likely to attract Gen Z consumers.

- Transparency and Authenticity: Transparency and authenticity are crucial for Gen Z. They seek out brands that are open about their practices, ingredients, and values. Authentic marketing and genuine brand stories resonate deeply with this generation.

2. Digital and Social Media Influence:

- Social Media Trends: Social media is a major influence on Gen Z's buying decisions. Platforms like Instagram, TikTok, and YouTube expose them to new products, trends, and brands. Viral trends and influencer endorsements can significantly impact their purchasing choices.

- Online Reviews and Ratings: Gen Z relies heavily on online reviews and ratings to inform their buying decisions. They trust peer reviews and user-generated content over traditional advertising, seeking out authentic feedback before making a purchase.

3. Convenience and Technology:

- E-Commerce and Mobile Shopping: E-commerce is a preferred shopping channel for Gen Z, who value the convenience and accessibility of online shopping. Mobile shopping, in particular, is popular, with many making purchases directly from their smartphones.

- Tech-Savvy Preferences: Tech-savvy and digitally native, Gen Z prefers brands that leverage technology to enhance the shopping experience. Features like personalized recommendations, AR try-ons, and seamless checkout processes appeal to their tech-forward mindset.

4. Personalization and Customization:

- Tailored Experiences: Gen Z appreciates personalized shopping experiences that cater to their individual preferences. Brands that use data and technology to offer tailored recommendations and customized products stand out in the competitive market.

- Self-Expression: Customizable products that allow for self-expression are particularly appealing to Gen Z. They seek out brands that offer unique, personalized options that reflect their identity and style.

Economic Impact of Gen Z's Buying Decisions

The buying decisions of Gen Z are reshaping various industries and influencing broader economic trends.

1. Retail and E-Commerce:

- Shift to Online Shopping: Gen Z's preference for online shopping is driving significant growth in the e-commerce sector. Retailers are investing in digital platforms, improving online user experiences, and expanding their delivery capabilities to meet this demand.

- Brick-and-Mortar Adaptations: Traditional brick-and-mortar stores are adapting to the digital preferences of Gen Z by incorporating technology into the in-store experience. Concepts like click-and-collect, in-store kiosks, and augmented reality are becoming more prevalent.

2. Sustainability and Ethical Practices:

- Pressure on Brands: Gen Z's demand for sustainability and ethical practices is putting pressure on brands to adopt greener and more responsible business practices. Companies are increasingly focusing on reducing their environmental footprint, ensuring ethical sourcing, and promoting social responsibility.

- Rise of Ethical Brands: Brands that prioritize sustainability and ethics are gaining market share. Gen Z's willingness to support these brands, even at a premium, is driving growth in the ethical consumerism sector.

3. Technology and Innovation:

- Investment in Tech Solutions: Gen Z's tech-savvy nature is pushing companies to invest in innovative solutions that enhance the customer experience. From AI-driven personalization to immersive AR and VR experiences, technology is becoming a key differentiator in the competitive market.

- Influence on Product Development: Companies are increasingly considering Gen Z's preferences in product development. Features like sustainability, customization, and tech integration are becoming standard expectations for new products.

4. Financial Services:

- Demand for Fintech Solutions: Gen Z's preference for convenience and digital solutions extends to financial services. Fintech companies are capitalizing on this by offering user-friendly, app-based solutions for banking, investing, and managing finances.

- Focus on Financial Education: Growing up during economic uncertainty has made financial education important for Gen Z. Financial institutions are developing educational content and tools to help this generation make informed financial decisions.

Strategies for Businesses to Engage Gen Z

To effectively engage Gen Z and tap into their purchasing power, businesses must understand their values and preferences and adapt their strategies accordingly.

1. Emphasize Sustainability and Ethics:

- Transparent Practices: Businesses should be transparent about their sustainability efforts and ethical practices. Clear communication about sourcing, production, and social impact can build trust and loyalty among Gen Z consumers.

- Sustainable Products: Developing and promoting sustainable products that align with Gen Z's values can attract their attention and drive sales. Highlighting eco-friendly materials, ethical sourcing, and environmental benefits is key.

2. Leverage Social Media and Influencers:

- Authentic Content: Creating authentic, relatable content that resonates with Gen Z is crucial. Collaborating with influencers who share the brand's values and appeal to Gen Z can amplify reach and credibility.

- Engagement and Interaction: Engaging with Gen Z on social media platforms through interactive content, live sessions, and real-time responses can build a strong online community and foster brand loyalty.

3. Enhance Digital and Mobile Shopping Experiences:

- Seamless E-Commerce: Ensuring a seamless e-commerce experience with user-friendly navigation, personalized recommendations, and efficient checkout processes is essential to meet Gen Z's expectations.

- Innovative Technology: Incorporating innovative technologies such as AR try-ons, virtual showrooms, and AI-driven personalization can enhance the shopping experience and differentiate the brand.

4. Offer Personalization and Customization:

- Tailored Recommendations: Using data analytics to offer personalized recommendations based on individual preferences and past behavior can create a more engaging shopping experience.

- Customizable Products: Providing options for product customization allows Gen Z to express their individuality and connect more deeply with the brand.

Generation Z's purchasing power and economic impact are significant and growing. Their unique preferences and values are reshaping markets, driving demand for sustainability, authenticity, and innovation. By understanding the factors that influence Gen Z's buying decisions and adapting strategies to meet their expectations, businesses can effectively engage this influential consumer group and capitalize on their economic potential. The rise of Gen Z as a major economic force heralds a new era of consumer behavior, characterized by a blend of digital savvy, value-driven consumption, and a demand for personalized, meaningful experiences.

Brand Loyalty and Expectations

Generation Z, born approximately between 1997 and 2012, represents a unique demographic with distinct preferences and expectations when it comes to brand loyalty. This chapter explores the factors that drive brand loyalty among Gen Z, their high expectations from brands, and how businesses can effectively engage and retain this influential consumer group.

Factors Driving Brand Loyalty in Gen Z

Gen Z's brand loyalty is influenced by a combination of values, experiences, and digital engagement. Understanding these factors is crucial for brands aiming to build and maintain loyalty among this generation.

1. Values Alignment:

   - Sustainability and Ethics: Gen Z places a high value on sustainability and ethical business practices. Brands that demonstrate a commitment to environmental responsibility, fair labor practices, and social justice are more likely to earn their loyalty.

- Authenticity and Transparency: Authenticity and transparency are key to building trust with Gen Z. They prefer brands that are honest about their practices, products, and values. Open communication and a genuine brand story resonate deeply with this demographic.

2. Personalized Experiences:

- Customization and Personalization: Gen Z values personalized experiences that cater to their individual preferences. Brands that offer customizable products or tailored recommendations based on their interests and behaviors can create a more engaging and satisfying shopping experience.

- Relevant and Timely Engagement: Engaging with Gen Z in a relevant and timely manner, whether through personalized marketing messages or responsive customer service, helps build a connection and fosters loyalty.

3. Digital Savvy and Innovation:

- Tech Integration: Gen Z appreciates brands that leverage technology to enhance the customer experience. Features such as mobile apps, augmented reality (AR), and virtual reality (VR) shopping experiences, and seamless online interfaces appeal to their tech-forward mindset.

- Social Media Presence: A strong and active social media presence is essential for connecting with Gen Z. Brands that engage with their audience through interactive content, influencer partnerships, and real-time responses can build a loyal following.

4. Community and Social Impact:

- Community Engagement: Brands that foster a sense of community and create spaces for Gen Z to connect with like-minded individuals can strengthen loyalty. This can include online forums, social media groups, or brand-hosted events.

- Social Responsibility: Demonstrating social responsibility through initiatives such as charitable donations, community support, and advocacy for important causes resonates with Gen Z and can enhance brand loyalty.

High Expectations from Brands

Gen Z's high expectations from brands are shaped by their digital upbringing, exposure to diverse choices, and strong values. Meeting these expectations is crucial for gaining and retaining their loyalty.

1. Quality and Value:

- High-Quality Products: Gen Z expects high-quality products that meet their needs and stand the test of time. They are willing to invest in brands that deliver superior quality and reliability.

- Value for Money: Value for money is important to Gen Z, who often balance quality with affordability.

Transparent pricing and a clear demonstration of the product's value can attract and retain their loyalty.

2. Seamless Customer Experience:

- Efficient and Convenient: A seamless and efficient customer experience, from browsing to checkout, is essential. Gen Z expects user-friendly websites, fast loading times, easy navigation, and quick delivery options.

- Responsive Customer Service: Responsive and helpful customer service, available through various channels such as live chat, social media, and email, is crucial for addressing their concerns and enhancing their overall experience.

3. Innovative and Engaging Marketing:

- Creative Content: Creative and engaging marketing content that captures their attention is key to appealing to Gen Z. This includes visually appealing graphics, entertaining videos, and interactive campaigns.

- Influencer Collaborations: Collaborations with influencers who align with their values and interests can amplify a brand's reach and credibility. Gen Z values the opinions of influencers they trust and follow.

4. Sustainability and Ethical Practices:

- Environmental Impact: Gen Z expects brands to minimize their environmental impact and adopt sustainable practices. This includes reducing waste, using eco-friendly materials, and promoting recycling and reusability.

- Ethical Labor Practices: Ethical labor practices, including fair wages, safe working conditions, and ethical sourcing, are important to Gen Z. Brands that prioritize the well-being of their workers can build trust and loyalty.

Strategies for Building and Maintaining Brand Loyalty

To effectively engage and retain Gen Z's loyalty, brands must adopt strategies that align with their values and expectations.

1. Authentic Storytelling:

- Genuine Brand Narratives: Brands should craft authentic narratives that reflect their values, mission

, and commitment to their customers. Sharing behind-the-scenes stories, the brand's journey, and the people behind the products can create a deeper connection with Gen Z.

2. Leveraging Technology:

- Enhanced Shopping Experiences: Utilize technology to create immersive and interactive shopping experiences. Augmented reality (AR) for virtual try-ons, artificial intelligence (AI) for personalized recommendations, and seamless mobile shopping apps can enhance the customer experience.

- Data-Driven Insights: Use data analytics to understand Gen Z's preferences and behaviors. Tailoring marketing strategies and product offerings based on these insights can increase relevance and engagement.

3. Engagement and Interaction:

- Active Social Media Presence: Maintain an active presence on social media platforms where Gen Z spends most of their time. Engage with them through interactive content, live sessions, and real-time responses to build a loyal community.

- Influencer Partnerships: Collaborate with influencers who resonate with Gen Z's values and interests. Authentic endorsements and collaborations can enhance credibility and reach.

4. Sustainability Initiatives:

- Environmental Commitment: Demonstrate a genuine commitment to sustainability through eco-friendly products, sustainable packaging, and transparent communication about environmental efforts. Highlighting these initiatives can attract environmentally conscious Gen Z consumers.

- Corporate Social Responsibility: Engage in corporate social responsibility (CSR) initiatives that align with causes important to Gen Z. Partnering with charities, supporting social justice movements, and participating in community projects can enhance brand loyalty.

5. Customer-Centric Approach:

- Feedback and Improvement: Actively seek feedback from Gen Z customers and use it to improve products and services. Showing that their opinions matter and implementing their suggestions can build trust and loyalty.

- Exceptional Customer Service: Provide exceptional customer service that is responsive, helpful, and available through multiple channels. Resolving issues quickly and effectively can enhance the overall customer experience.

6. Personalization and Customization:

- Tailored Marketing: Use personalized marketing strategies to deliver relevant content and offers. Email campaigns, targeted ads, and personalized recommendations based on browsing history and preferences can increase engagement.

- Customizable Products: Offer products that can be customized to reflect individual preferences. Gen Z values uniqueness and the ability to express their identity through personalized products.

7. Creating Community:

- Brand Communities: Foster a sense of community around the brand through online forums, social media groups, and brand-hosted events. Encouraging interaction among customers can create a loyal and engaged community.

- User-Generated Content: Encourage customers to create and share content related to the brand. User-generated content, such as reviews, photos, and videos, can enhance authenticity and build a sense of community.

Case Studies of Brands Succeeding with Gen Z

Examining successful brands can provide valuable insights into effective strategies for building and maintaining brand loyalty among Gen Z.

1. Patagonia:

- Sustainability Focus: Patagonia's commitment to environmental sustainability and ethical practices has resonated deeply with Gen Z. Their transparent communication about their environmental impact and initiatives to reduce it have built strong loyalty.

- Activism and Advocacy: Patagonia's active involvement in environmental activism and advocacy aligns with Gen Z's values, further strengthening their connection to the brand.

2. Glossier:

- Community Engagement: Glossier's emphasis on community engagement and user-generated content has made them a favorite among Gen Z. Their approach to involving customers in product development and valuing their feedback fosters loyalty.

- Authentic Marketing: Glossier's authentic and relatable marketing, often featuring real customers and their stories, appeals to Gen Z's preference for authenticity.

3. Nike:

- Influencer Collaborations: Nike's strategic collaborations with influencers and athletes who resonate with Gen Z have boosted their brand appeal. These partnerships create relatable and aspirational connections.

- Innovative Technology: Nike's use of technology, such as the Nike Training Club app and AR features in their mobile app, enhances the customer experience and aligns with Gen Z's tech-savvy expectations.

Brand loyalty among Generation Z is driven by a combination of values alignment, personalized experiences, digital engagement, and community involvement. Brands that can meet Gen Z's high expectations for sustainability, authenticity, innovation, and customer-centricity are more likely to build and maintain loyalty. By adopting strategies that resonate with Gen Z's preferences and leveraging successful case studies, businesses can effectively engage this influential consumer group and foster long-term loyalty. Understanding and responding to the unique drivers of Gen Z's brand loyalty is essential for brands aiming to thrive in an evolving marketplace.

The Role of Online Reviews and Recommendations

For Generation Z, born approximately between 1997 and 2012, online reviews and recommendations play a pivotal role in shaping their purchasing decisions. This chapter delves into how Gen Z interacts with and relies on online reviews, the influence of peer and influencer recommendations, and the implications for businesses seeking to attract and retain this digital-native generation.

The Importance of Online Reviews

Online reviews are a critical component of the decision-making process for Gen Z consumers. They provide valuable insights, build trust, and influence perceptions of products and services.

1. Trust and Credibility:

- Peer Reviews: Gen Z places a high level of trust in peer reviews, often viewing them as more credible than traditional advertising. Authentic, user-generated reviews provide real-world insights that help them gauge the quality and reliability of a product or service.

- Verified Purchases: Reviews marked as "verified purchase" hold even more weight, as they indicate that the reviewer has genuinely used the product. This additional layer of authenticity further reinforces trust.

2. Detailed Information:

- Comprehensive Insights: Online reviews often contain detailed information about the product's performance, usability, and value. Gen Z relies on these comprehensive insights to make informed decisions, comparing different products and evaluating their features and benefits.

- Pros and Cons: Reviews that outline both the positive and negative aspects of a product help Gen Z weigh their options. Balanced feedback allows them to consider potential drawbacks and make a more nuanced purchasing decision.

3. Social Proof:

- Popularity Indicators: A high number of positive reviews serves as social proof, indicating that a product is popular and well-regarded. Gen Z is influenced by this collective approval and is more likely to choose products with substantial positive feedback.

- Community Validation: Reviews create a sense of community validation, where the opinions of others in their age group or with similar interests provide reassurance about the purchase.

The Influence of Recommendations

In addition to online reviews, recommendations from peers, influencers, and social media play a significant role in Gen Z's buying decisions.

1. Peer Recommendations:

- Word of Mouth: Recommendations from friends and family are highly valued by Gen Z. Personal endorsements from trusted individuals carry significant weight and can strongly influence their purchasing choices.

- Social Media Sharing: Gen Z often shares and seeks recommendations through social media platforms. Whether it's a tweet about a new product or a post on Instagram, these recommendations reach a broad audience and can drive purchasing behavior.

2. Influencer Recommendations:

- Influencer Partnerships: Influencers who resonate with Gen Z's values and interests have a powerful impact on their buying decisions. Collaborations between brands and influencers can effectively reach this audience and build trust through authentic endorsements.

- Micro-Influencers: Micro-influencers, who have smaller but highly engaged followings, are particularly effective in influencing Gen Z. Their recommendations feel more personal and relatable, fostering a sense of trust and connection.

3. User-Generated Content:

- Authentic Content: User-generated content, such as unboxing videos, product reviews, and testimonials, provides authentic perspectives that Gen Z values. This type of content often feels more genuine and trustworthy than brand-generated content.

- Interactive Engagement: Platforms that encourage user-generated content, such as YouTube, TikTok, and Instagram, enable Gen Z to engage with brands and products in interactive and meaningful ways. This engagement can drive interest and loyalty.

Strategies for Leveraging Reviews and Recommendations

To effectively leverage online reviews and recommendations, businesses need to adopt strategies that resonate with Gen Z's preferences and behaviors.

1. Encouraging Authentic Reviews:

- Simplifying the Review Process: Making it easy for customers to leave reviews by streamlining the process can increase the number of authentic reviews. Simple prompts and reminders after a purchase can encourage feedback.

- Incentivizing Reviews: Offering incentives, such as discounts on future purchases or entry into a giveaway, can motivate customers to leave reviews. However, it's essential to ensure that these incentives don't compromise the authenticity of the feedback.

2. Engaging with Reviewers:

- Responding to Reviews: Actively responding to both positive and negative reviews demonstrates that a brand values customer feedback and is committed to continuous improvement. This engagement can build trust and loyalty.

- Addressing Concerns: Addressing negative reviews professionally and constructively shows that a brand is willing to resolve issues and prioritize customer satisfaction. This proactive approach can mitigate negative perceptions and turn dissatisfied customers into advocates.

3. Leveraging Influencer Partnerships:

- Authentic Collaborations: Partnering with influencers who genuinely use and appreciate the brand can create more authentic and impactful endorsements. These collaborations should align with the influencer's content style and audience interests.

- Long-Term Relationships: Building long-term relationships with influencers, rather than one-off promotions, can enhance credibility and foster deeper connections with their followers. Consistent and genuine endorsements are more effective in building trust.

4. Utilizing User-Generated Content:

- Showcasing Customer Experiences: Highlighting user-generated content on brand websites and social media channels can provide authentic and relatable perspectives. Featuring customer photos, videos, and reviews creates a sense of community and trust.

- Encouraging Content Creation: Encouraging customers to share their experiences with branded hashtags or through contests can generate valuable user-generated content. This content can amplify the brand's reach and influence through organic engagement.

Case Studies of Brands Successfully Leveraging Reviews and Recommendations

Examining successful brands provides insights into effective strategies for leveraging online reviews and recommendations to engage Gen Z.

1. Glossier:

- Community-Driven Approach: Glossier's community-driven approach encourages customers to share their experiences and feedback. The brand actively engages with its community on social media, highlighting user-generated content and responding to reviews.

- Transparency and Authenticity: Glossier's transparency about product ingredients and development processes builds trust with Gen Z. The brand's emphasis on authentic reviews and customer experiences has fostered a loyal following.

2. Warby Parker:

- Customer-Centric Reviews: Warby Parker leverages customer reviews and testimonials to build trust and credibility. The brand features detailed customer feedback on its website, helping potential buyers make informed decisions.

- Engaging Customer Service: Warby Parker's responsive customer service team addresses reviews and concerns promptly, demonstrating a commitment to customer satisfaction and building a positive reputation.

3. Nike:

- Influencer Collaborations: Nike's strategic collaborations with influencers and athletes resonate with Gen Z. These partnerships highlight authentic product use and experiences, reinforcing the brand's credibility and appeal.

- Interactive Social Media Campaigns: Nike engages with its audience through interactive social media campaigns that encourage user-generated content. Hashtags like JustDoIt invite customers to share their fitness journeys, creating a sense of community and trust.

Online reviews and recommendations are integral to Gen Z's purchasing decisions. They rely on authentic feedback from peers, influencers, and user-generated content to make informed choices. Brands that effectively leverage these elements by encouraging authentic reviews, engaging with reviewers, and building genuine influencer partnerships can build trust and loyalty among Gen Z consumers. Understanding the critical role of online reviews and recommendations is essential for businesses aiming to connect with and influence this digital-native generation. By adopting strategies that resonate with Gen Z's preferences and behaviors, brands can successfully navigate the digital landscape and foster lasting loyalty.

CHAPTER 08

MARKETING TO GEN Z

Effective Strategies for Engaging Gen Z

Generation Z, born approximately between 1997 and 2012, represents a unique demographic with distinct preferences, behaviors, and values. As the first true digital natives, their expectations and interactions with brands are shaped by their constant connectivity and exposure to diverse content. This chapter explores effective strategies for engaging Gen Z, focusing on authenticity, social media, personalization, and values-driven marketing.

Understanding Gen Z

Before delving into specific strategies, it's essential to understand the core characteristics of Gen Z that influence their consumer behavior.

1. Digital Natives:

- Tech-Savvy: Gen Z has grown up with smartphones, social media, and instant access to information. They are adept at navigating digital platforms and have high expectations for seamless, tech-driven experiences.

- Multi-Platform Usage: They frequently use multiple devices and platforms, from smartphones and tablets to gaming consoles and smart TVs. Their multitasking ability means they consume content across various channels simultaneously.

2. Value-Driven:

- Socially Conscious: Gen Z values social justice, sustainability, and ethical business practices. They prefer brands that align with their values and demonstrate a commitment to positive social impact.

- Authenticity: Authenticity is crucial for Gen Z. They seek genuine, transparent communication from brands and are quick to spot and reject insincerity or inauthenticity.

3. Short Attention Spans:

- Quick Content Consumption: Gen Z is accustomed to fast-paced, bite-sized content. They have short attention spans and are selective about what captures their interest.

- Engagement Over Intrusion: Traditional advertising methods are often viewed as intrusive. Gen Z prefers interactive and engaging content that offers value or entertainment.

Effective Strategies for Engaging Gen Z

To effectively engage Gen Z, brands need to adopt strategies that resonate with their preferences and behaviors. The following approaches can help capture their attention and build lasting connections.

1. Embrace Authenticity and Transparency:

- Honest Communication: Brands should communicate openly and honestly about their products, practices, and values. Transparency builds trust and credibility with Gen Z.

- Showcase Real Stories: Highlight real customer stories, employee experiences, and behind-the-scenes content. Authentic narratives resonate more with Gen Z than polished marketing messages.

2. Leverage Social Media:

- Platform-Specific Strategies: Understand the unique dynamics of each social media platform. For instance, Instagram is great for visually appealing content, TikTok for short, engaging videos, and Twitter for real-time interactions.

- Influencer Collaborations: Partner with influencers who align with the brand's values and appeal to Gen Z. Authentic influencer endorsements can amplify reach and credibility.

- Interactive Content: Create interactive content such as polls, quizzes, challenges, and live streams. Engagement-driven content encourages participation and fosters a sense of community.

3. Prioritize Personalization:

- Tailored Experiences: Use data and analytics to personalize marketing efforts. Tailored recommendations, personalized emails, and customized shopping experiences can enhance relevance and engagement.

- Dynamic Content: Implement dynamic content that adapts based on user preferences and behavior. This approach can make interactions more meaningful and increase conversion rates.

4. Focus on Video Content:

- Short-Form Videos: Leverage platforms like TikTok, Instagram Reels, and YouTube Shorts to create short, impactful videos. These formats align with Gen Z's content consumption habits.

- Authentic Video Marketing: Use videos to tell authentic stories, showcase product demonstrations, and provide tutorials. High-quality, genuine video content can capture attention and drive engagement.

5. Highlight Social Responsibility:

- Sustainable Practices: Communicate the brand's commitment to sustainability and ethical practices. Highlight eco-friendly products, sustainable sourcing, and initiatives to reduce environmental impact.

- Social Impact Initiatives: Showcase involvement in social impact initiatives and community projects. Gen Z is more likely to support brands that actively contribute to positive change.

6. Create Community and Foster Engagement:

- Online Communities: Build and nurture online communities where Gen Z can connect with like-minded individuals. Brand-hosted forums, social media groups, and community events can create a sense of belonging.

- User-Generated Content: Encourage customers to create and share content related to the brand. User-generated content, such as reviews, photos, and videos, enhances authenticity and fosters community engagement.

7. Utilize Innovative Technology:

- Augmented Reality (AR): Implement AR features for virtual try-ons, interactive product demos, and immersive brand experiences. AR can enhance the shopping experience and provide unique engagement opportunities.

- Artificial Intelligence (AI): Use AI-driven personalization to deliver tailored recommendations and predictive insights. AI can help create more relevant and personalized interactions with Gen Z consumers.

8. Engage Through Purpose-Driven Marketing:

- Align with Causes: Align the brand with causes that resonate with Gen Z's values, such as climate change, social justice, and mental health. Purpose-driven marketing can create emotional connections and drive loyalty.

- Storytelling with Purpose: Use storytelling to convey the brand's mission and impact. Highlighting the brand's purpose and contributions to society can inspire and engage Gen Z.

Case Studies of Brands Succeeding with Gen Z

Examining successful brands provides insights into effective strategies for engaging Gen Z.

1. Nike:

- Authentic Campaigns: Nike's "Dream Crazy" campaign featuring Colin Kaepernick resonated with Gen Z by addressing social justice issues and promoting authenticity. The campaign's bold stance aligned with Gen Z's values and garnered widespread support.

- Interactive Experiences: Nike's use of technology, such as the Nike Training Club app and AR features, enhances the customer experience and engages Gen Z with personalized, interactive content.

2. Glossier:

- Community-Driven Approach: Glossier's emphasis on community engagement and user-generated content has made it a favorite among Gen Z. The brand involves its community in product development and values authentic customer feedback.

- Influencer Collaborations: Glossier's collaborations with micro-influencers who genuinely use and love their products have created authentic endorsements and built trust with Gen Z consumers.

3. Starbucks:

- Sustainability Initiatives: Starbucks' commitment to sustainability, such as reducing plastic waste and supporting ethical sourcing, resonates with Gen Z's environmental values. The brand's transparent communication about these efforts builds trust.

- Personalization and Technology: Starbucks leverages technology for personalized experiences, such as the Starbucks app, which offers tailored recommendations, rewards, and mobile ordering.

Engaging Generation Z requires a deep understanding of their unique preferences, values, and behaviors. Brands that embrace authenticity, leverage social media, prioritize personalization, highlight social responsibility, and create interactive, community-driven experiences are more likely to capture the attention and loyalty of Gen Z consumers. By adopting these strategies and learning from successful brands, businesses can effectively navigate the digital landscape and build lasting connections with this influential generation.

Understanding and responding to Gen Z's expectations is essential for brands aiming to thrive in an ever-evolving marketplace.

Content Creation: Authenticity and Relatability

Generation Z, born approximately between 1997 and 2012, has grown up in a world saturated with digital content. As a result, they have developed a keen ability to discern between genuine and inauthentic messaging. For brands looking to engage this demographic, creating content that is both authentic and relatable is crucial. This chapter explores the importance of authenticity and relatability in content creation, and provides strategies for effectively connecting with Gen Z.

The Importance of Authenticity

Authenticity is a cornerstone of effective marketing to Gen Z. This generation values honesty and transparency, and they are quick to dismiss content that feels contrived or disingenuous.

1. Trust and Credibility:

- Honest Communication: Gen Z expects brands to be honest about their products, values, and business practices.

Authentic communication builds trust and credibility, which are essential for fostering long-term loyalty.

- Real Stories: Sharing real stories about the brand's journey, the people behind the products, and customer experiences can enhance authenticity. Gen Z appreciates brands that are open and honest about their successes and challenges.

2. Transparency:

- Behind-the-Scenes Content: Behind-the-scenes content provides a glimpse into the brand's operations, culture, and values. This transparency helps humanize the brand and fosters a deeper connection with Gen Z.

- Ethical Practices: Being transparent about sourcing, production, and sustainability practices is crucial. Gen Z values brands that are open about their efforts to operate ethically and sustainably.

The Power of Relatability

Relatability is equally important in content creation for Gen Z. Content that reflects their experiences, interests, and values resonates more deeply and fosters a sense of connection.

1. Understanding the Audience:

- Cultural Relevance: Understanding the cultural context and interests of Gen Z is essential for creating relatable content. This includes staying up-to-date with trends, slang, and the issues that matter to them.

- Shared Experiences: Content that reflects shared experiences, such as navigating school, work, or social relationships, can create a sense of solidarity and connection with Gen Z.

2. Inclusive Representation:

- Diverse Voices: Featuring diverse voices and perspectives in content is crucial for relatability. Gen Z values inclusivity and wants to see themselves and their communities represented authentically.

- Authentic Portrayals: Avoiding stereotypes and presenting authentic portrayals of different cultures, genders, and identities enhances relatability and shows respect for the audience.

Strategies for Creating Authentic and Relatable Content

To create content that resonates with Gen Z, brands need to adopt strategies that prioritize authenticity and relatability. The following approaches can help achieve this.

1. User-Generated Content (UGC):

- Encouraging UGC: Encouraging customers to create and share content related to the brand can enhance authenticity. User-generated content, such as reviews, photos, and videos, provides genuine perspectives that resonate with Gen Z.

- Showcasing UGC: Featuring user-generated content on brand websites and social media channels can create a sense of community and trust. Highlighting real customers' experiences adds authenticity to the brand's messaging.

2. Influencer Collaborations:

- Authentic Partnerships: Collaborating with influencers who genuinely use and appreciate the brand can create authentic endorsements. Influencers who align with the brand's values and appeal to Gen Z can enhance credibility.

- Micro-Influencers: Partnering with micro-influencers who have smaller but highly engaged followings can create more personal and relatable connections. Their endorsements often feel more genuine and trustworthy.

3. Storytelling:

- Narrative Content: Using storytelling to convey the brand's mission, values, and impact can create emotional connections. Stories that highlight real people and real experiences resonate deeply with Gen Z.

- Empathy and Emotion: Content that evokes empathy and emotion can make a lasting impact. Sharing stories of overcoming challenges, making a difference, or personal growth can inspire and engage Gen Z.

4. Interactive Content:

- Engagement-Driven Content: Creating interactive content such as polls, quizzes, and challenges encourages participation and engagement. Gen Z enjoys content that allows them to interact and express their opinions.

- Real-Time Interaction: Leveraging live streams, Q&A sessions, and interactive videos can create real-time connections with the audience. This immediate interaction enhances authenticity and relatability.

5. Humor and Creativity:

- Humorous Content: Incorporating humor into content can make it more relatable and enjoyable for Gen Z. Memes, funny videos, and lighthearted posts can capture their attention and create a positive association with the brand.

- Creative Formats: Experimenting with creative formats, such as short-form videos, animations, and graphics, can make content more engaging and visually appealing. Creativity in content presentation can set the brand apart and resonate with Gen Z's aesthetic preferences.

Case Studies of Successful Content Strategies

Examining successful brands provides insights into effective strategies for creating authentic and relatable content for Gen Z.

1. Dove:

- Real Beauty Campaign: Dove's Real Beauty campaign features real women of different ages, sizes, and ethnicities, promoting body positivity and self-acceptance. This authentic representation resonates with Gen Z's values of inclusivity and self-love.

- User-Generated Content: Dove encourages users to share their own stories and experiences with the brand, creating a sense of community and authenticity.

2. Chipotle:

- Engaging Social Media: Chipotle's social media content includes memes, humor, and user-generated content, making it relatable and entertaining for Gen Z. The brand's playful and authentic approach has garnered a strong following.

- Interactive Campaigns: Chipotle engages with its audience through interactive campaigns, such as TikTok challenges and Instagram polls, encouraging participation and fostering a sense of community.

3. Nike:

- Inspirational Storytelling: Nike's storytelling approach, featuring athletes and individuals overcoming challenges, creates emotional connections. The brand's campaigns, such as "Dream Crazy," resonate with Gen Z's values of perseverance and social justice.

- Influencer Partnerships: Nike's collaborations with influencers and athletes who authentically align with the brand's message enhance credibility and relatability.

Creating authentic and relatable content is essential for engaging Generation Z. By prioritizing transparency, inclusivity, and genuine storytelling, brands can build trust and foster deep connections with this demographic. Leveraging strategies such as user-generated content, influencer collaborations, interactive content, and creative formats can enhance authenticity and relatability. Understanding and responding to Gen Z's preferences and values is crucial for brands aiming to thrive in a rapidly evolving digital landscape. By adopting these strategies, businesses can effectively capture the attention and loyalty of Gen Z, fostering long-term success.

The Power of Influencer Marketing

Influencer marketing has become one of the most effective strategies for engaging Generation Z, born approximately between 1997 and 2012. This demographic, known for its digital savviness and skepticism towards traditional advertising, places a high value on authenticity and peer recommendations. Influencers, who often feel like trusted peers, play a crucial role in shaping Gen Z's buying decisions. This chapter explores the power of influencer marketing, how it resonates with Gen Z, and strategies for leveraging it effectively.

The Influence of Influencers

Influencers are individuals with the ability to affect the opinions, behaviors, and purchasing decisions of their followers due to their authority, knowledge, position, or relationship with their audience. For Gen Z, influencers are more than just content creators; they are relatable figures who provide trusted recommendations.

1. Authenticity and Trust:

- Relatable Figures: Influencers often share their personal lives, challenges, and successes, making them relatable to their followers. This authenticity builds trust and fosters a sense of connection that traditional advertisements cannot replicate.

- Genuine Recommendations: Influencers who genuinely use and endorse products provide credible and trustworthy recommendations. Gen Z values these authentic endorsements over polished, scripted ads.

2. Peer Influence:

- Social Proof: Seeing influencers use and recommend products provides social proof that can significantly impact Gen Z's purchasing decisions. If a trusted influencer endorses a product, their followers are more likely to consider it.

- Community and Belonging: Influencers often cultivate a sense of community among their followers. Gen Z feels part of a larger group with shared interests and values, reinforcing their trust in the influencer's recommendations.

3. Diverse Content:

- Variety of Platforms: Influencers create content across multiple platforms, including Instagram, YouTube, TikTok, and Twitter. This multi-platform presence allows brands to reach Gen Z where they spend their time.

- Engaging Formats: Influencers use various content formats, such as videos, live streams, stories, and posts, to engage their audience. This diversity keeps the content fresh and engaging, catering to Gen Z's preference for dynamic media.

Effective Strategies for Influencer Marketing

To effectively leverage influencer marketing for engaging Gen Z, brands need to adopt strategies that align with their preferences and behaviors. The following approaches can help maximize the impact of influencer collaborations.

1. Choosing the Right Influencers:

- Alignment with Brand Values: Select influencers whose values and content align with the brand's mission and message. Authentic alignment enhances credibility and ensures that the influencer's audience is a good fit for the brand.

- Engagement Over Follower Count: Focus on influencers with high engagement rates rather than just large follower counts. Influencers with active, engaged audiences are more likely to drive meaningful interactions and conversions.

2. Fostering Authentic Collaborations:

- Genuine Partnerships: Develop genuine partnerships with influencers, allowing them to create content that reflects their authentic experiences with the brand. Avoid overly scripted or controlled content that can appear inauthentic.

- Long-Term Relationships: Building long-term relationships with influencers can create more sustained and impactful collaborations. Consistent endorsements over time strengthen trust and loyalty among the influencer's followers.

3. Creating Engaging Content:

- Interactive Campaigns: Design interactive campaigns that encourage audience participation. Challenges, giveaways, and Q&A sessions can boost engagement and create a sense of involvement.

- Storytelling: Encourage influencers to tell stories about their experiences with the brand. Storytelling adds depth to the content and makes it more relatable and memorable for Gen Z.

4. Utilizing Micro-Influencers:

- Targeted Reach: Micro-influencers, who have smaller but highly engaged followings, can be particularly effective in niche markets. Their recommendations often feel more personal and trustworthy.

- Cost-Effective: Collaborating with multiple micro-influencers can be more cost-effective than partnering with a single mega-influencer, while still achieving significant reach and impact.

5. Measuring Impact and ROI:

- Analytics and Insights: Use analytics tools to track the performance of influencer campaigns. Metrics such as engagement rates, reach, and conversions provide insights into the campaign's effectiveness.

- Adjusting Strategies: Based on the insights gained, adjust influencer marketing strategies to optimize future campaigns. Continuous improvement ensures that the brand remains aligned with Gen Z's evolving preferences.

Case Studies of Successful Influencer Marketing

Examining successful brands provides insights into effective strategies for leveraging influencer marketing to engage Gen Z.

1. Fenty Beauty:

- Diverse Influencer Partnerships: Fenty Beauty, founded by Rihanna, collaborates with a diverse range of influencers, reflecting the brand's commitment to inclusivity. This approach resonates deeply with Gen Z's values of diversity and representation.

- Authentic Content: Influencers share genuine reviews and tutorials using Fenty Beauty products, providing authentic and relatable content that builds trust and credibility.

2. Gymshark:

- Community Building: Gymshark has built a strong community by partnering with fitness influencers who embody the brand's ethos. These influencers engage with their followers through workout routines, fitness tips, and motivational content.

- Interactive Campaigns: Gymshark's influencer campaigns often include challenges and interactive elements, encouraging participation and fostering a sense of community among followers.

3. Daniel Wellington:

- Strategic Gifting: Daniel Wellington's strategy of gifting watches to influencers has led to widespread, authentic endorsements. Influencers sharing their genuine appreciation for the products has driven brand awareness and sales.

- User-Generated Content: The brand encourages users to share photos wearing their watches with branded hashtags. This user-generated content amplifies the reach and authenticity of influencer campaigns.

Influencer marketing is a powerful tool for engaging Generation Z. Influencers provide authentic, relatable recommendations that resonate deeply with this demographic. By choosing the right influencers, fostering genuine collaborations, creating engaging content, and utilizing micro-influencers, brands can effectively leverage the power of influencer marketing. Successful case studies from brands like Fenty Beauty, Gymshark, and Daniel Wellington demonstrate the impact of strategic influencer partnerships. Understanding and embracing the nuances of influencer marketing is essential for brands aiming to capture the attention and loyalty of Gen Z in a competitive digital landscape.

CHAPTER 09

THE FUTURE OF GEN Z IN THE WORKFORCE

Career Aspirations and Work Preferences

As Generation Z, born approximately between 1997 and 2012, begins to enter the workforce, their unique perspectives and preferences are set to reshape the professional landscape. This chapter explores the career aspirations and work preferences of Gen Z, examining the factors that influence their career choices, the qualities they seek in employers, and how they envision their professional futures.

Career Aspirations

Generation Z's career aspirations are influenced by their values, experiences, and the socio-economic environment in which they have grown up. Understanding these aspirations is essential for employers looking to attract and retain top Gen Z talent.

1. Value-Driven Careers:

- Purpose and Impact: Gen Z seeks careers that provide a sense of purpose and the opportunity to make a positive impact on society. They are drawn to roles and organizations that align with their values, such as sustainability, social justice, and community development.

- Ethical and Sustainable Companies: They prefer working for companies that demonstrate a commitment to ethical practices and sustainability. Transparency about corporate social responsibility (CSR) initiatives and environmental efforts is crucial.

2. Entrepreneurial Spirit:

- Desire for Independence: Many Gen Z individuals aspire to entrepreneurial careers, valuing the independence and flexibility that comes with running their own businesses. They are attracted to the idea of being their own boss and creating something unique.

- Side Hustles and Freelancing: Even those pursuing traditional careers often engage in side hustles or freelancing. This entrepreneurial mindset allows them to explore their passions and diversify their income streams.

3. Emphasis on Work-Life Balance:

- Flexibility: Work-life balance is a top priority for Gen Z. They seek flexible work arrangements, such as remote work, flexible hours, and the ability to manage their schedules in a way that supports their personal lives.

- Mental Health and Well-Being: Gen Z is highly aware of the importance of mental health and well-being. They prioritize employers who offer support for mental health, such as wellness programs, mental health days, and a positive work environment.

4. Continuous Learning and Development:

- Professional Growth: Gen Z values opportunities for continuous learning and professional development. They seek employers who provide training, mentorship, and clear pathways for career advancement.

- Skill Development: They are interested in roles that allow them to develop a diverse set of skills and stay adaptable in a rapidly changing job market. Access to resources for upskilling and reskilling is important.

Work Preferences

Understanding Gen Z's work preferences can help employers create environments that attract and retain this talented generation.

1. Technologically Integrated Workplaces:

- Digital Tools and Platforms: As digital natives, Gen Z expects workplaces to be equipped with the latest technology and digital tools. They are comfortable using various platforms for communication, collaboration, and project management.

- Remote and Hybrid Work: The preference for remote and hybrid work models is strong among Gen Z. They appreciate the flexibility and autonomy that remote work provides, along with the opportunity to balance work with other aspects of their lives.

2. Collaborative and Inclusive Cultures:

- Team Collaboration: Gen Z thrives in collaborative environments where teamwork and open communication are encouraged. They value diverse perspectives and enjoy working with others to solve problems and achieve common goals.

- Inclusivity and Diversity: Inclusivity and diversity are non-negotiable for Gen Z. They expect workplaces to foster a culture of inclusivity, where everyone feels valued and respected, regardless of their background.

3. Transparent and Ethical Leadership:

- Open Communication: Gen Z prefers leaders who are transparent, approachable, and open to feedback. They appreciate regular communication about company goals, performance, and changes.

- Ethical Leadership: Integrity and ethical behavior are crucial qualities they look for in leaders. They want to work for leaders who act responsibly and prioritize the well-being of employees and the community.

4. Recognition and Feedback:

- Frequent Feedback: Gen Z values regular feedback and recognition for their work. They appreciate knowing how they are performing and where they can improve. Constructive feedback helps them grow and stay motivated.

- Achievement Recognition: Recognizing achievements, both big and small, is important for maintaining morale and motivation. They appreciate acknowledgment of their contributions and efforts.

Preparing for the Future Workforce

Employers can take several steps to attract and retain Gen Z talent by aligning their practices with Gen Z's career aspirations and work preferences.

1. Creating Purpose-Driven Roles:

- Aligning Roles with Values: Design roles that align with the values and aspirations of Gen Z. Highlight how these roles contribute to the company's mission and positive societal impact.

- CSR Initiatives: Promote the company's CSR initiatives and demonstrate a genuine commitment to making a difference. Show how employees can be involved in these efforts.

2. Fostering a Flexible Work Environment:

- Remote Work Options: Provide options for remote and hybrid work arrangements. Equip employees with the necessary tools and support to work effectively from any location.

- Flexible Hours: Implement flexible working hours to accommodate different lifestyles and personal commitments. Trust employees to manage their schedules and deliver results.

3. Investing in Learning and Development:

- Training Programs: Offer comprehensive training programs that support continuous learning and professional growth. Provide access to courses, workshops, and certification programs.

- Mentorship Opportunities: Establish mentorship programs that connect Gen Z employees with experienced professionals. Mentorship can provide guidance, support, and valuable insights for career development.

4. Promoting a Collaborative and Inclusive Culture:

- Team-Building Activities: Organize team-building activities that promote collaboration and camaraderie. Encourage cross-functional projects and open communication channels.

- Diversity Initiatives: Implement initiatives that promote diversity and inclusivity. Ensure that hiring practices, policies, and company culture reflect a commitment to inclusivity.

5. Offering Competitive Benefits:

- Health and Wellness Programs: Provide comprehensive health and wellness programs that support physical and mental well-being. Include benefits such as gym memberships, mental health resources, and wellness workshops.

- Recognition Programs: Develop recognition programs that celebrate employee achievements and contributions. Regularly acknowledge and reward hard work and innovation.

Case Studies of Companies Succeeding with Gen Z

Examining successful companies provides insights into effective strategies for attracting and retaining Gen Z talent.

1. Google:

- Innovative Work Environment: Google offers an innovative and flexible work environment with remote work options and state-of-the-art technology. Their commitment to employee well-being and continuous learning makes them attractive to Gen Z.

- Inclusive Culture: Google's emphasis on diversity and inclusion, along with initiatives such as employee resource groups and mentorship programs, aligns with Gen Z's values.

2. Salesforce:

-        Purpose-Driven Mission: Salesforce's commitment to social responsibility and sustainability resonates with Gen Z. The company's efforts to give back to communities and promote environmental sustainability attract purpose-driven candidates.

- Employee Development: Salesforce invests in employee development through extensive training programs and career advancement opportunities. Their focus on continuous learning appeals to Gen Z's desire for growth.

3. Adobe:

- Flexibility and Work-Life Balance: Adobe offers flexible work arrangements, including remote work options and flexible hours. Their commitment to work-life balance and employee well-being aligns with Gen Z's priorities.

- Recognition and Feedback: Adobe's culture of regular feedback and recognition supports employee growth and motivation. Their transparent and supportive leadership style resonates with Gen Z.

Generation Z's career aspirations and work preferences are reshaping the future of the workforce. They seek value-driven careers, prioritize work-life balance, and desire continuous learning and development. Employers that understand and align with these preferences can attract and retain top Gen Z talent by creating purpose-driven roles, fostering a flexible and inclusive work environment, and investing in employee growth and well-being. Understanding Gen Z's unique perspective is essential for building a future-ready workforce that thrives in a rapidly evolving professional landscape.

Remote Work and the Gig Economy

Generation Z, born approximately between 1997 and 2012, is entering the workforce with distinct preferences shaped by the digital age. Two significant trends that resonate with this generation are remote work and the gig economy. This chapter explores how these trends align with Gen Z's career aspirations and work preferences, the benefits and challenges associated with each, and strategies for employers to effectively integrate these models into their workplaces.

The Appeal of Remote Work

Remote work has become increasingly popular, particularly in the wake of the COVID-19 pandemic. For Gen Z, remote work offers numerous advantages that align with their values and lifestyle.

1. Flexibility and Autonomy:

- Work-Life Balance: Remote work allows Gen Z to achieve a better work-life balance. They can manage their schedules more effectively, accommodating personal commitments and reducing commute-related stress.

- Independence: Gen Z values autonomy and the ability to work independently. Remote work provides the freedom to choose their work environment and conditions, fostering a sense of control and self-management.

2. Technological Integration:

- Comfort with Digital Tools: As digital natives, Gen Z is highly comfortable using various digital tools and platforms for communication, collaboration, and project management. This makes remote work a natural fit for them.

- Innovation and Efficiency: Remote work environments often leverage innovative technologies to enhance productivity and efficiency. Gen Z is adept at utilizing these tools to optimize their workflow.

3. Geographical Flexibility:

- Global Opportunities: Remote work opens up opportunities to work for companies worldwide, breaking down geographical barriers. This aligns with Gen Z's desire for diverse experiences and global exposure.

- Cost of Living: The ability to work remotely allows Gen Z to live in areas with a lower cost of living while still accessing job opportunities in higher-cost regions.

The Gig Economy

The gig economy, characterized by short-term, flexible jobs or freelance work, is another appealing option for Gen Z. This model offers unique benefits that cater to their career aspirations and work preferences.

1. Entrepreneurial Opportunities:

- Side Hustles: Many Gen Z individuals engage in side hustles, leveraging their skills and interests to generate additional income. The gig economy supports this entrepreneurial spirit, providing platforms to monetize various talents.

- Business Ventures: The gig economy allows Gen Z to test entrepreneurial ventures with minimal risk. Freelancing and gig work can serve as stepping stones to launching their own businesses.

2. Diverse Work Experiences:

- Skill Development: Gig work offers opportunities to work on diverse projects and roles, helping Gen Z develop a broad skill set. This variety keeps work interesting and supports continuous learning.

- Networking: Engaging in different gigs enables Gen Z to build a diverse professional network, opening doors to future opportunities and collaborations.

3. Work-Life Integration:

- Flexible Schedules: The gig economy offers flexibility in choosing work hours and projects, allowing Gen Z to integrate work with their personal lives seamlessly.

- Remote Possibilities: Many gig jobs can be done remotely, combining the benefits of remote work with the flexibility of the gig economy.

Benefits and Challenges

While remote work and the gig economy offer significant advantages, they also present challenges that Gen Z and employers must navigate.

1. Benefits:

- Increased Productivity: Remote work can lead to increased productivity as employees can create optimal work environments and schedules that suit their needs.

- Job Satisfaction: Flexibility and autonomy in remote work and gig jobs contribute to higher job satisfaction, as employees feel more in control of their careers.

- Work-Life Balance: Both remote work and gig economy models support a better work-life balance, reducing burnout and improving overall well-being.

2. Challenges:

- Isolation: Remote work can lead to feelings of isolation and disconnection from colleagues. Employers must find ways to foster a sense of community and belonging.

- Job Security: Gig work often lacks the job security and benefits associated with traditional employment. This can create financial instability and uncertainty for workers.

- Time Management: The flexibility of remote and gig work requires strong time management skills. Without structure, some individuals may struggle to maintain productivity and balance.

Strategies for Employers

To effectively integrate remote work and the gig economy into their workplaces, employers can adopt several strategies that align with Gen Z's preferences and needs.

1. Supporting Remote Work:

- Digital Infrastructure: Invest in robust digital infrastructure that supports remote work, including secure communication platforms, project management tools, and cloud-based systems.

- Remote Work Policies: Develop clear remote work policies that outline expectations, performance metrics, and communication protocols. This provides structure and clarity for remote employees.

- Virtual Engagement: Foster virtual engagement through regular team meetings, virtual social events, and collaboration tools. Building a strong virtual community helps mitigate feelings of isolation.

2. Leveraging the Gig Economy:

- Flexible Work Models: Offer flexible work models that include gig and freelance opportunities. This allows Gen Z to engage with the company in various capacities while maintaining flexibility.

- Project-Based Hiring: Consider project-based hiring for specific tasks or short-term projects. This approach allows the company to tap into diverse talent pools and bring in specialized skills as needed.

- Fair Compensation: Ensure fair compensation and timely payments for gig workers. Providing competitive rates and financial stability can attract top talent.

3. Supporting Career Development:

- Training and Resources: Offer training and resources to help remote and gig workers develop their skills and advance their careers. Access to online courses, workshops, and mentorship programs can support continuous learning.

- Performance Feedback: Provide regular performance feedback and recognition. Constructive feedback helps remote and gig workers understand their strengths and areas for improvement, fostering professional growth.

4. Promoting Work-Life Balance:

- Mental Health Support: Implement mental health support programs, such as counseling services, wellness workshops, and mental health days. Supporting employees' well-being is crucial for maintaining productivity and satisfaction.

- Flexible Scheduling: Allow flexible scheduling options to accommodate personal commitments and promote work-life balance. Trust employees to manage their time effectively and deliver results.

Case Studies of Successful Implementation

Examining companies that have successfully integrated remote work and the gig economy provides insights into effective strategies for engaging Gen Z.

1. Shopify:

- Remote-First Approach: Shopify has adopted a remote-first approach, allowing employees to work from anywhere. The company provides robust digital infrastructure and virtual engagement initiatives to support remote work.

- Employee Well-Being: Shopify emphasizes employee well-being through mental health support, flexible scheduling, and wellness programs, aligning with Gen Z's values.

2. Upwork:

- Freelance Marketplace: Upwork operates as a freelance marketplace, providing gig opportunities for professionals across various fields. The platform supports

Gen Z's entrepreneurial spirit and desire for diverse work experiences.

   - Skill Development: Upwork offers resources and training for freelancers to enhance their skills and succeed in the gig economy. This focus on professional growth appeals to Gen Z's continuous learning mindset.

   3. Slack:

   - Collaboration Tools: Slack provides a collaboration platform that supports remote work and virtual engagement. The company's tools facilitate communication and teamwork, addressing the challenges of remote work.

   - Inclusive Culture: Slack promotes an inclusive culture through diversity initiatives, virtual social events, and employee resource groups. This approach resonates with Gen Z's values of inclusivity and community.

   Generation Z's career aspirations and work preferences are driving the adoption of remote work and the gig economy. These models offer flexibility, autonomy, and opportunities for entrepreneurial ventures, aligning with Gen Z's values and lifestyle. While they present challenges such as isolation and job security, employers can effectively integrate these models by investing in digital infrastructure, supporting career development, and promoting work-life balance. Understanding and responding to Gen Z's preferences is essential for building a future-ready workforce that thrives in a rapidly evolving professional landscape.

Leadership and Innovation: Gen Z's Impact on Business

As Generation Z, born approximately between 1997 and 2012, begins to enter the workforce, their unique perspectives, skills, and values are poised to drive significant changes in business leadership and innovation. This chapter explores how Gen Z is shaping the future of business, the qualities they bring to leadership roles, their approach to innovation, and the implications for companies seeking to harness their potential.

Gen Z's Leadership Qualities

Gen Z brings distinct qualities to leadership roles, influenced by their digital upbringing, value-driven mindset, and emphasis on inclusivity and collaboration.

1. Digital Fluency:

- Tech-Savvy Leaders: Gen Z leaders are digital natives who are highly proficient with technology. They seamlessly integrate digital tools and platforms into their leadership practices, enhancing efficiency and communication.

- Data-Driven Decision Making: This generation values data and analytics, using these tools to make informed decisions and drive business strategies. Their ability to analyze and interpret data positions them as effective leaders in the digital age.

2. Inclusive and Collaborative Leadership:

- Emphasis on Diversity: Gen Z leaders prioritize diversity and inclusivity, recognizing the value of diverse perspectives and experiences. They strive to create inclusive environments where everyone feels valued and respected.

- Collaborative Approach: Rather than top-down management, Gen Z favors a collaborative approach to leadership. They seek to empower their teams, encourage open communication, and foster a culture of teamwork and mutual support.

3. Value-Driven Leadership:

- Ethical and Transparent: Integrity and transparency are core to Gen Z's leadership style. They lead with honesty, ethical behavior, and a commitment to doing what is right for their employees, customers, and communities.

- Purpose-Driven Missions: Gen Z leaders are motivated by purpose and seek to align their organizations with meaningful missions. They focus on creating positive social and environmental impact through their business practices.

4. Adaptability and Resilience:

- Embracing Change: Growing up in a rapidly changing world, Gen Z leaders are adaptable and open to change. They are not afraid to challenge the status quo and experiment with new ideas and approaches.

- Resilience in Adversity: Gen Z has shown resilience in the face of economic and social challenges. This resilience translates into their leadership, where they demonstrate the ability to navigate uncertainty and inspire their teams during difficult times.

Gen Z's Approach to Innovation

Gen Z's innovative mindset is transforming how businesses operate, develop products, and engage with customers. Their approach to innovation is characterized by creativity, collaboration, and a focus on solving real-world problems.

1. Technology-Driven Innovation:

- Leveraging Emerging Technologies: Gen Z is quick to adopt and leverage emerging technologies such as artificial intelligence, blockchain, and the Internet of Things (IoT). They use these technologies to drive innovation and create competitive advantages.

- Digital Transformation: Gen Z leaders are spearheading digital transformation initiatives, modernizing business processes, and enhancing customer experiences through digital solutions.

2. Customer-Centric Innovation:

- Understanding Customer Needs: Gen Z places a strong emphasis on understanding and addressing customer needs. They use data and customer feedback to inform product development and improve user experiences.

- Personalization: Innovation efforts are often focused on personalization, creating tailored experiences that resonate with individual customers. Gen Z uses technology to deliver customized products and services that meet specific preferences and requirements.

3. Sustainable Innovation:

- Environmental Responsibility: Sustainability is a key driver of innovation for Gen Z. They prioritize eco-friendly practices and develop sustainable products and processes that minimize environmental impact.

- Circular Economy: Gen Z leaders are exploring and implementing circular economy models, focusing on reducing waste and promoting the reuse and recycling of materials.

4. Collaborative Innovation:

- Cross-Functional Teams: Gen Z values collaboration and often forms cross-functional teams to drive innovation. They recognize the importance of diverse expertise and perspectives in generating creative solutions.

- Open Innovation: Open innovation, involving collaboration with external partners such as startups, academic institutions, and customers, is a common approach. Gen Z leaders seek to harness collective intelligence and co-create value.

Implications for Businesses

The impact of Gen Z on leadership and innovation has significant implications for businesses. Companies must adapt to harness the potential of this generation effectively.

1. Cultivating Gen Z Leaders:

- Leadership Development Programs: Implement leadership development programs tailored to Gen Z's strengths and values. Focus on digital skills, ethical leadership, and inclusivity to prepare them for leadership roles.

- Mentorship and Support: Provide mentorship and support networks to help Gen Z leaders navigate their careers. Experienced leaders can offer guidance and share insights to foster their growth and development.

2. Fostering an Innovative Culture:

- Encouraging Creativity: Create an environment that encourages creativity and experimentation. Allow employees to explore new ideas, take risks, and learn from failures without fear of repercussions.

- Investing in Technology: Invest in the latest technologies and digital tools that enable innovation. Provide the resources and infrastructure needed for Gen Z to drive technological advancements and digital transformation.

3. Embracing Inclusivity and Diversity:

- Inclusive Policies: Implement policies and practices that promote diversity and inclusion at all levels of the organization. Ensure that all employees feel valued and have equal opportunities to contribute and advance.

- Diverse Teams: Build diverse teams that bring a range of perspectives and experiences to the table. This diversity enhances creativity and innovation, driving better decision-making and problem-solving.

4. Aligning with Values:

- Purpose-Driven Strategies: Develop business strategies that align with Gen Z's values of social and environmental responsibility. Clearly communicate the company's mission and demonstrate a commitment to making a positive impact.

- Ethical Practices: Ensure that business practices are ethical and transparent. Gen Z expects companies to operate with integrity and prioritize the well-being of their employees, customers, and communities.

Case Studies of Gen Z's Impact on Business

Examining companies where Gen Z is making a significant impact provides insights into how this generation is driving leadership and innovation.

1. Patagonia:

- Sustainable Leadership: Patagonia, known for its commitment to environmental sustainability, has embraced Gen Z leaders who prioritize eco-friendly practices. Their leadership has driven innovations in sustainable product design and supply chain management.

- Activism and Advocacy: Patagonia's involvement in environmental activism and advocacy resonates with Gen Z's values. The company's purpose-driven mission attracts and retains Gen Z talent.

2. Tesla:

- Technological Innovation: Tesla's focus on technological innovation aligns with Gen Z's strengths. Gen Z leaders and employees at Tesla are driving advancements in electric vehicles, renewable energy, and autonomous driving technology.

- Sustainability Focus: Tesla's mission to accelerate the world's transition to sustainable energy appeals to Gen Z's commitment to environmental responsibility. The company's innovative products reflect this focus.

3. Google:

- Inclusive Leadership: Google fosters an inclusive leadership culture that empowers Gen Z leaders. Initiatives such as employee resource groups and diversity training support this inclusivity.

- Digital Transformation: Google's emphasis on digital transformation and innovation aligns with Gen Z's skills and values. The company's projects in AI, cloud computing, and digital advertising reflect their innovative mindset.

Generation Z's entry into the workforce is driving significant changes in business leadership and innovation. Their digital fluency, inclusive approach, value-driven mindset, and adaptability make them effective leaders and innovators. Businesses that recognize and harness the potential of Gen Z can benefit from their fresh perspectives and innovative ideas. By cultivating Gen Z leaders, fostering an innovative culture, embracing inclusivity, and aligning with values, companies can thrive in a rapidly evolving business landscape. Understanding and leveraging Gen Z's impact on leadership and innovation is essential for building a future-ready organization.

CHAPTER 10

THE GLOBAL PERSPECTIVE

Cultural Differences and Similarities

Generation Z, born approximately between 1997 and 2012, is the most connected and globally aware generation to date. While this cohort shares many similarities across different regions due to their digital upbringing, there are also notable cultural differences influenced by local contexts. This chapter explores the cultural differences and similarities of Gen Z around the world, examining how these factors influence their values, behaviors, and expectations.

Shared Characteristics of Gen Z

Despite cultural differences, Gen Z shares several common traits globally, shaped by their exposure to digital technology and the internet.

1. Digital Natives:

- Tech-Savvy: Gen Z across the world is adept at using digital technology. They have grown up with smartphones, social media, and instant access to information, making them highly proficient in navigating digital platforms.

- Social Media Engagement: Social media is a unifying factor for Gen Z, with platforms like Instagram, TikTok, and YouTube playing a significant role in their daily lives. They use these platforms to connect, share, and consume content.

2. Value-Driven:

- Social Justice: Gen Z globally is passionate about social justice issues, including equality, diversity, and human rights. They are vocal about their beliefs and use digital platforms to advocate for change.

- Environmental Concerns: Environmental sustainability is a critical concern for Gen Z everywhere. They are aware of the impact of climate change and prioritize eco-friendly practices and products.

3. Educational Aspirations:

- Importance of Education: Education is highly valued by Gen Z across different cultures. They see it as a pathway to personal and professional success and are eager to learn and acquire new skills.

- Lifelong Learning: Gen Z embraces lifelong learning, utilizing online courses, tutorials, and resources to continuously develop their knowledge and skills.

Cultural Differences

While there are many similarities, cultural differences among Gen Z are shaped by local traditions, societal norms, and economic conditions.

1. Family and Community:

- Collectivist vs. Individualist Cultures: In collectivist cultures, such as those in many Asian and African countries, Gen Z places a strong emphasis on family and community. They value group harmony and often prioritize family obligations over personal ambitions. In contrast, in individualist cultures, like those in the United States and Western Europe, Gen Z is more focused on personal achievements and individual expression.

- Intergenerational Relationships: In some cultures, intergenerational relationships are highly valued, with Gen Z showing great respect for elders and seeking their guidance. In others, Gen Z tends to be more independent and less reliant on family for decision-making.

2. Work and Career Aspirations:

- Job Stability vs. Flexibility: In regions with high economic uncertainty, such as parts of Eastern Europe and Latin America, Gen Z often prioritizes job stability and security. In contrast, in economically stable regions, like North America and Western Europe, Gen Z may prioritize job flexibility and opportunities for personal growth over long-term job security.

- Entrepreneurial Spirit: While the entrepreneurial spirit is common among Gen Z globally, its manifestation can vary. In some regions, starting a business may be driven by necessity due to limited job opportunities, whereas in others, it may be driven by innovation and the desire for independence.

3. Social and Political Engagement:

- Activism: The forms of activism and the issues that resonate with Gen Z can differ. For instance, in Western countries, Gen Z may focus on climate change and gender equality, while in regions with political instability, such as parts of the Middle East and Africa, they may be more concerned with political freedom and human rights.

- Use of Social Media for Activism: The role of social media in activism can vary based on internet accessibility and censorship. In countries with high internet penetration and freedom of expression, social media is a powerful tool for activism. In contrast, in regions with restricted internet access, Gen Z may find alternative ways to advocate for change.

4. Consumer Behavior:

- Brand Loyalty: Cultural attitudes toward brand loyalty can differ. In some cultures, Gen Z may show strong loyalty to established brands that have a longstanding reputation. In others, they may be more open to experimenting with new and innovative brands.

- Sustainable Consumption: While environmental concerns are common, the emphasis on sustainable consumption can vary. In developed regions, there may be a stronger focus on purchasing eco-friendly products, while in developing regions, affordability and necessity may take precedence over sustainability.

Strategies for Businesses to Navigate Cultural Differences

For businesses aiming to engage Gen Z globally, understanding and navigating cultural differences is crucial. Here are strategies to consider:

1. Localized Marketing:

- Cultural Sensitivity: Develop marketing campaigns that are culturally sensitive and resonate with local values and norms. Avoid one-size-fits-all approaches and tailor messages to reflect the unique characteristics of each region.

- Language and Communication: Use local languages and culturally relevant communication styles. This can enhance relatability and ensure that the message is effectively conveyed.

2. Inclusive Branding:

- Diverse Representation: Ensure that marketing materials feature diverse representation that reflects the local population. This inclusivity can build trust and appeal to Gen Z's value for diversity.

- Authenticity: Authentic branding that genuinely reflects the company's values and mission resonates across cultures. Avoid superficial gestures and demonstrate a real commitment to the issues that matter to Gen Z.

3. Community Engagement:

- Local Partnerships: Partner with local influencers, organizations, and communities to build credibility and trust. These partnerships can provide valuable insights and help businesses connect with Gen Z in meaningful ways.

- Support Local Initiatives: Support local social and environmental initiatives that align with Gen Z's values. This can enhance the brand's reputation and demonstrate a commitment to positive impact.

4. Adapting Products and Services:

- Customization: Adapt products and services to meet the specific needs and preferences of different regions. This customization can enhance relevance and appeal to local Gen Z consumers.

- Accessibility: Ensure that products and services are accessible and affordable for Gen Z in different economic contexts. Consider local economic conditions and purchasing power when setting prices.

Case Studies of Cultural Adaptation

Examining successful brands provides insights into how cultural adaptation can effectively engage Gen Z globally.

1. Nike:

- Localized Campaigns: Nike has successfully launched localized campaigns that reflect the cultural nuances of different regions. For example, their "Just Do It" campaign in China featured local athletes and highlighted issues relevant to Chinese Gen Z, such as academic pressure and family expectations.

- Diverse Representation: Nike's commitment to diversity and inclusion is evident in its global campaigns, which feature athletes and influencers from various backgrounds, reflecting the diversity of Gen Z.

2. Coca-Cola:

- Cultural Sensitivity: Coca-Cola's marketing strategies are highly culturally sensitive, often incorporating local traditions, festivals, and languages. Their "Share a Coke" campaign, which personalized bottles with local names, resonated deeply with Gen Z across different cultures.

- Community Engagement: Coca-Cola supports numerous local community initiatives and sustainability projects, demonstrating a commitment to positive impact and aligning with Gen Z's values.

3. Adidas:

- Global and Local Balance: Adidas strikes a balance between maintaining a global brand identity and adapting to local markets. Their campaigns often blend global themes with local relevance, such as collaborations with local designers and influencers.

- Sustainability Focus: Adidas's emphasis on sustainability, such as their use of recycled materials in products, appeals to Gen Z's environmental concerns globally, while localizing their sustainability efforts to address specific regional issues.

Generation Z, while sharing many global characteristics due to their digital upbringing, also exhibits significant cultural differences shaped by local contexts. Understanding these differences and similarities is crucial for businesses aiming to engage this influential generation. By adopting strategies that emphasize cultural sensitivity, inclusivity, and local relevance, companies can effectively connect with Gen Z and harness their potential. Navigating the global landscape requires a nuanced approach that respects and celebrates the diversity of Gen Z, ultimately fostering stronger connections and driving success in the global market.

The Influence of Global Events on Gen Z

Generation Z, born approximately between 1997 and 2012, has grown up in a world marked by rapid change and significant global events. These events have profoundly influenced their perspectives, values, and behaviors. This chapter explores how global events have shaped Gen Z, examining their impact on this generation's worldview, social activism, mental health, and consumer behavior.

The Impact of Major Global Events

Several major global events have left a lasting imprint on Gen Z, influencing their collective consciousness and shaping their approach to various aspects of life.

1. The COVID-19 Pandemic:

- Health Awareness: The pandemic has heightened Gen Z's awareness of health and wellness. They are more conscientious about personal hygiene, mental health, and the importance of healthcare systems.

- Digital Transformation: COVID-19 accelerated the shift to digital platforms for education, work, and social interactions. Gen Z adapted quickly to online learning, remote work, and virtual socializing, further embedding technology into their daily lives.

- Economic Uncertainty: The economic repercussions of the pandemic, including job losses and financial instability, have made Gen Z more cautious about their financial futures. They value job security and are keen on financial planning and saving.

2. Climate Change and Environmental Crises:

- Environmental Activism: Witnessing the tangible effects of climate change, such as extreme weather events and environmental degradation, has galvanized Gen Z to advocate for environmental sustainability. They participate in climate strikes, support eco-friendly brands, and push for systemic change.

- Sustainable Living: Gen Z prioritizes sustainable living practices, including reducing waste, conserving resources, and supporting green technologies. They expect businesses to adopt sustainable practices and are willing to pay a premium for eco-friendly products.

3. Social Justice Movements:

- Equality and Inclusion: Movements such as Black Lives Matter, MeToo, and LGBTQ+ rights have deeply resonated with Gen Z. They are passionate about equality and inclusion, actively participating in protests, campaigns, and social media activism.

- Corporate Responsibility: Gen Z holds businesses accountable for their social impact. They expect companies to take a stand on social justice issues, implement inclusive practices, and contribute to positive societal change.

4. Political Polarization and Unrest:

- Civic Engagement: Political polarization and unrest in various regions have driven Gen Z to become more politically active and informed. They engage in political discourse, vote in elections, and advocate for policies that align with their values.

- Global Perspective: Exposure to global political issues, such as immigration, human rights, and international relations, has broadened Gen Z's worldview. They are more likely to consider the global implications of local events and policies.

5. Technological Advancements:

- Adaptation to New Technologies: Growing up with rapid technological advancements, Gen Z is adept at adopting new technologies and integrating them into their lives. They are early adopters of innovations such as artificial intelligence, blockchain, and virtual reality.

- Digital Privacy and Security: Increased reliance on digital platforms has made Gen Z more aware of privacy and security issues. They are cautious about data sharing and expect companies to prioritize data protection and transparency.

The Response of Gen Z to Global Events

Gen Z's response to global events is characterized by proactive engagement, adaptability, and a strong sense of responsibility.

1. Social Activism and Advocacy:

- Grassroots Movements: Gen Z is at the forefront of grassroots movements, organizing protests, campaigns, and community initiatives. They use social media to mobilize support, raise awareness, and effect change.

- Collaborative Efforts: Collaboration is a hallmark of Gen Z's activism. They work with peers, organizations, and influencers to amplify their impact and create a collective voice for change.

2. Mental Health and Well-Being:

- Increased Awareness: Global events have heightened Gen Z's awareness of mental health issues. They prioritize mental well-being, seek professional help, and advocate for mental health support and resources.

- Coping Mechanisms: Gen Z employs various coping mechanisms to manage stress and anxiety, such as mindfulness practices, physical activity, and digital detoxes. They also rely on online communities and support groups for emotional support.

3. Educational and Career Choices:

- Reskilling and Upskilling: Economic uncertainty and technological advancements have motivated Gen Z to pursue continuous learning and skill development. They prioritize education and seek opportunities to reskill and upskill to remain competitive in the job market.

- Purpose-Driven Careers: Influenced by global events, Gen Z is drawn to careers that align with their values and allow them to make a positive impact. They seek roles in sustainability, social justice, healthcare, and technology.

4. Consumer Behavior:

- Conscious Consumption: Gen Z's consumer behavior is heavily influenced by their values. They support brands that demonstrate ethical practices, sustainability, and social responsibility. They also prefer products that offer transparency and authenticity.

- Digital Shopping: The pandemic accelerated the shift to online shopping, a trend that Gen Z has embraced. They value convenience, variety, and the ability to research products and read reviews online before making a purchase.

Strategies for Engaging Gen Z in a Post-Global Event World

Businesses and organizations must adapt their strategies to effectively engage Gen Z, considering the profound impact of global events on this generation.

1. Emphasizing Authenticity and Transparency:

   - Honest Communication: Communicate openly and honestly about the company's practices, values, and impact. Gen Z values transparency and is quick to discern inauthenticity.

   - Showcasing Real Impact: Highlight real stories and tangible impacts of the company's efforts in areas such as sustainability, social justice, and community support. Use data and evidence to back up claims.

2. Supporting Social and Environmental Causes:

   - Corporate Social Responsibility (CSR): Implement robust CSR programs that address social and environmental issues. Involve Gen Z in these initiatives and communicate the outcomes and benefits.

   - Partnerships and Collaborations: Partner with organizations, influencers, and communities that align with Gen Z's values. Collaborative efforts can enhance credibility and amplify impact.

3. Promoting Mental Health and Well-Being:

   - Workplace Support: Create a supportive work environment that prioritizes mental health and well-being. Offer resources such as counseling, wellness programs, and flexible work arrangements.

   - Community Engagement: Support mental health initiatives in the broader community. Engage in campaigns and programs that raise awareness and provide support for mental health issues.

4. Fostering Innovation and Adaptability:

- Investing in Technology: Invest in cutting-edge technologies and digital tools that enhance the customer experience and streamline operations. Gen Z appreciates innovation and efficiency.

- Encouraging Creativity: Foster a culture of creativity and experimentation. Encourage employees to explore new ideas, take risks, and learn from failures.

Case Studies of Gen Z's Response to Global Events

Examining how Gen Z has responded to global events provides insights into their values, behaviors, and expectations.

1. Fridays for Future:

- Climate Activism: Founded by Greta Thunberg, Fridays for Future is a global movement led by Gen Z to demand action on climate change. The movement has organized worldwide climate strikes, raising awareness and pushing for policy changes.

- Youth Leadership: The movement demonstrates Gen Z's leadership in environmental activism and their ability to mobilize global support for pressing issues.

2. Black Lives Matter:

- Social Justice Advocacy: Gen Z has played a significant role in the Black Lives Matter movement, advocating for racial equality and justice. They use social media to amplify voices, organize protests, and educate others about systemic racism.

- Corporate Accountability: The movement has pressured companies to address diversity and inclusion, leading to tangible changes in corporate policies and practices.

3. Mental Health Awareness Campaigns:

- Breaking Stigmas: Gen Z has been instrumental in breaking the stigma around mental health. They actively participate in mental health awareness campaigns, share personal experiences, and advocate for better mental health resources.

- Online Support: Online platforms and communities provide a space for Gen Z to discuss mental health issues openly and seek support from peers and professionals.

Global events have profoundly influenced Generation Z, shaping their values, behaviors, and expectations. From the COVID-19 pandemic and climate change to social justice movements and technological advancements, these events have left an indelible mark on this generation. Gen Z's proactive engagement, adaptability, and strong sense of responsibility are driving significant changes in how they approach social activism, mental health, education, careers, and consumer behavior. Understanding and responding to the impact of global events on Gen Z is essential for businesses, organizations, and society to effectively engage and support this influential generation in a rapidly changing world.

Case Studies from Different Regions

Generation Z, born approximately between 1997 and 2012, is a globally connected generation that exhibits both shared characteristics and unique cultural nuances influenced by their local environments. This chapter delves into specific case studies from different regions around the world, illustrating how Gen Z's behaviors, values, and responses to global events are shaped by their cultural contexts.

North America: United States

1. Climate Activism and Sustainability:

- Case Study: The Sunrise Movement: The Sunrise Movement is a youth-led political movement in the United States that advocates for climate action and the Green New Deal. Founded by young activists, the movement has garnered significant support from Gen Z, who are passionate about environmental sustainability and combating climate change.

- Impact: The Sunrise Movement has influenced public discourse and policy-making, pushing for aggressive climate policies at the federal level. Their activism reflects Gen Z's commitment to sustainability and their willingness to engage in political advocacy.

2. Social Justice and Inclusion:

- Case Study: Black Lives Matter (BLM): The BLM movement, which gained prominence after the killing of Trayvon Martin in 2012, has seen substantial involvement from Gen Z. Young Americans have played a key role in organizing protests, raising awareness on social media, and advocating for systemic change to address racial injustice.

- Impact: The movement has led to increased awareness and dialogue about racial inequality in the United States, influencing changes in corporate policies, law enforcement practices, and educational curricula.

3. Digital Innovation and Entrepreneurship:

- Case Study: TikTok Influencers: TikTok has become a significant platform for Gen Z in the United States, providing opportunities for digital entrepreneurship. Influencers like Charli D'Amelio and Addison Rae have built massive followings, turning their online presence into profitable careers through brand partnerships and merchandise.

- Impact: The success of TikTok influencers underscores Gen Z's entrepreneurial spirit and their ability to leverage digital platforms for economic opportunities. It also highlights the shift towards new forms of media consumption and content creation.

Europe: United Kingdom

1. Mental Health Advocacy:

- Case Study: YoungMinds: YoungMinds is a leading charity in the UK dedicated to improving the mental health of young people. Gen Z has been actively involved in both utilizing and supporting the charity's services, advocating for better mental health resources and awareness.

- Impact: The increased focus on mental health has led to greater availability of mental health services in schools and communities, as well as a broader public dialogue about mental health issues. This reflects Gen Z's prioritization of mental well-being.

2. Political Engagement and Activism:

- Case Study: Brexit: The Brexit referendum and subsequent political developments have deeply impacted Gen Z in the UK. Many young people were opposed to leaving the European Union, fearing negative repercussions on their future opportunities and the country's diversity.

- Impact: Gen Z's political engagement has increased, with many becoming more involved in politics and advocacy to influence future policy decisions. This engagement demonstrates their desire to shape their socio-political environment.

3. Sustainable Fashion:

- Case Study: Depop: Depop is a social shopping app that has gained popularity among Gen Z in the UK for buying and selling second-hand and vintage fashion. The platform combines social media elements with e-commerce, allowing users to create and share their own fashion styles.

- Impact: Depop's success highlights Gen Z's commitment to sustainable consumption and their innovative approach to fashion. It also reflects their desire for unique, personalized shopping experiences.

Asia: China

1. Technological Integration:

- Case Study: ByteDance and Douyin: Douyin, the Chinese counterpart of TikTok, has become immensely popular among Gen Z in China. ByteDance, the parent company, has created a platform that blends entertainment, social interaction, and e-commerce.

- Impact: Douyin's integration of social media and e-commerce has transformed digital consumption habits in China. Gen Z's engagement with the platform showcases their adaptability to new technologies and their influence on market trends.

2. Educational Aspirations:

- Case Study: Gaokao Pressure: The Gaokao, China's national college entrance exam, is a significant event for Gen Z students. The intense competition and pressure to perform well in the exam reflect the high value placed on education in Chinese society.

- Impact: The focus on educational achievement has led to high levels of academic stress but also to significant investments in educational resources and tutoring services. It highlights Gen Z's dedication to academic success and future career opportunities.

3. Social Media and E-Commerce:

- Case Study: KOLs (Key Opinion Leaders): In China, Key Opinion Leaders (KOLs) have a significant influence on Gen Z's consumer behavior. Platforms like Weibo, WeChat, and Little Red Book are popular channels where KOLs share content and endorse products.

- Impact: KOLs drive trends and purchasing decisions, illustrating Gen Z's trust in peer recommendations and influencer marketing. This trend reflects the merging of social media and commerce in China's digital economy.

Africa: Nigeria

1. Entrepreneurial Spirit:

- Case Study: Tech Startups: Nigeria's tech ecosystem is burgeoning, with many young entrepreneurs leading the charge. Companies like Paystack and Flutterwave, founded by young Nigerians, are revolutionizing the fintech industry in Africa.

- Impact: The rise of tech startups highlights Gen Z's entrepreneurial drive and their ability to create innovative solutions to local challenges. This entrepreneurial spirit is contributing to economic growth and job creation in Nigeria.

2. Social Activism:

- Case Study: EndSARS Movement: The EndSARS movement, which protests against police brutality in Nigeria, has seen significant participation from Gen Z. Young Nigerians have utilized social media to organize protests, share information, and demand government accountability.

- Impact: The movement has raised global awareness about police brutality in Nigeria and has led to government promises of reform. It demonstrates Gen Z's commitment to social justice and their ability to mobilize for change.

3. Cultural Preservation and Innovation:

- Case Study: Afrobeat Music: The global popularity of Afrobeat music, with artists like Burna Boy and Wizkid, reflects Gen Z's role in preserving and promoting Nigerian culture. These artists have gained international acclaim while staying true to their cultural roots.

- Impact: The success of Afrobeat music highlights Gen Z's influence in the global cultural landscape and their ability to innovate within traditional cultural frameworks. It also showcases the importance of cultural identity to Gen Z in Nigeria.

Latin America: Brazil

1. Environmental Advocacy:

- Case Study: Amazon Rainforest Protection: Gen Z in Brazil is deeply concerned about the deforestation of the Amazon rainforest. Young activists, such as indigenous youth leaders, are at the forefront of efforts to protect the rainforest and raise awareness about environmental issues.

- Impact: These advocacy efforts have brought international attention to the plight of the Amazon and have pressured the Brazilian government to take action. It reflects Gen Z's commitment to environmental sustainability and indigenous rights.

2. Digital Creativity:

- Case Study: Digital Content Creators: Brazilian Gen Z is highly active on social media platforms like YouTube, Instagram, and TikTok, where they create and share diverse content, from comedy and music to social commentary.

- Impact: The popularity of Brazilian digital content creators underscores Gen Z's creativity and their ability to influence cultural trends both locally and globally. It also highlights their role in shaping digital entertainment.

3. Political Engagement:

- Case Study: Youth Political Movements: In recent years, Brazil has seen a rise in youth-led political movements advocating for issues such as education, corruption, and human rights. Gen Z is increasingly involved in these movements, using social media to organize and spread their messages.

- Impact: These political movements have led to increased youth participation in elections and policy discussions, demonstrating Gen Z's desire to influence their country's political future. It highlights their commitment to civic engagement and democratic processes.

Generation Z's behaviors, values, and responses to global events are shaped by a complex interplay of shared global experiences and unique cultural contexts. These case studies from different regions illustrate the diverse ways in which Gen Z is influencing and being influenced by their local environments. Understanding these regional differences and similarities is crucial for businesses, organizations, and policymakers aiming to engage and support this dynamic generation. By recognizing and respecting the cultural nuances that shape Gen Z, stakeholders can foster stronger connections and effectively address the needs and aspirations of this globally aware and active generation.

CHAPTER 11

CHALLENGES AND OPPORTUNITIES

Navigating Mental Health Issues

Generation Z, born approximately between 1997 and 2012, faces unique mental health challenges influenced by their upbringing in a digitally connected and rapidly changing world. While they are more open about discussing mental health compared to previous generations, they also experience high levels of stress, anxiety, and depression. This chapter explores the mental health issues prevalent among Gen Z, the factors contributing to these challenges, and the strategies and opportunities for effectively addressing and navigating mental health.

Prevalence of Mental Health Issues

Research and surveys consistently show that mental health issues are a significant concern for Gen Z.

1. High Rates of Anxiety and Depression:

- Statistics: Studies indicate that Gen Z reports higher levels of anxiety and depression compared to previous generations. Factors such as academic pressure, economic uncertainty, and social media influence contribute to these high rates.

- Self-Reporting: Gen Z is more likely to self-report mental health issues and seek help, reflecting a growing awareness and destigmatization of mental health.

2. Stress and Burnout:

- Academic and Career Pressures: The pressure to excel academically and secure stable, well-paying jobs is a significant source of stress for Gen Z. This pressure is exacerbated by competitive environments and high expectations.

- Constant Connectivity: The always-on nature of digital communication can lead to burnout. Gen Z feels the need to stay constantly connected, often blurring the lines between personal and academic or work-related time.

Contributing Factors

Several factors contribute to the mental health challenges faced by Gen Z, ranging from technological influences to societal expectations.

1. Digital Overload:

- Social Media: While social media provides opportunities for connection and self-expression, it also contributes to feelings of inadequacy, loneliness, and cyberbullying. The curated nature of social media can create unrealistic standards and comparisons.

- Screen Time: Excessive screen time, especially before bedtime, can disrupt sleep patterns and contribute to mental health issues. Gen Z's reliance on digital devices for both leisure and work exacerbates this problem.

2. Economic Uncertainty:

- Financial Stress: Economic instability, student debt, and the uncertainty of job markets contribute to financial stress among Gen Z. Concerns about affordability of higher education, housing, and living expenses are prevalent.

- Job Insecurity: The changing nature of work, with the rise of gig economies and automation, creates anxiety about job security and career prospects.

3. Academic and Social Pressures:

- High Expectations: Gen Z faces high expectations from parents, educators, and society to achieve academically and professionally. This pressure can lead to chronic stress and anxiety.

- Social Isolation: Despite being digitally connected, many Gen Z individuals experience social isolation. The decline in face-to-face interactions and the impact of events like the COVID-19 pandemic have exacerbated feelings of loneliness.

4. Global Events and Uncertainty:

- Pandemic Impact: The COVID-19 pandemic has had a profound impact on mental health, with increased isolation, uncertainty, and disruption of daily routines. Gen Z has faced significant challenges in adapting to these changes.

- Climate Anxiety: Concerns about climate change and the future of the planet contribute to a sense of anxiety and helplessness. Gen Z is acutely aware of environmental issues and the long-term impact on their lives.

Strategies for Addressing Mental Health Issues

Addressing the mental health challenges faced by Gen Z requires a multifaceted approach involving individuals, families, educational institutions, workplaces, and policymakers.

1. Promoting Mental Health Awareness:

- Education and Training: Integrate mental health education into school curriculums and workplace training programs. Increasing awareness and understanding of mental health issues can reduce stigma and encourage help-seeking behavior.

- Public Campaigns: Launch public health campaigns to raise awareness about mental health and available resources. Utilize social media and digital platforms to reach Gen Z effectively.

2. Enhancing Access to Mental Health Services:

- Affordable and Accessible Care: Ensure that mental health services are affordable and accessible to all, regardless of socioeconomic status. Expand insurance coverage for mental health treatments and provide low-cost or free options for those in need.

- Telehealth and Digital Solutions: Leverage telehealth and digital platforms to provide remote mental health services. Online therapy, counseling, and mental health apps can offer convenient and effective support.

3. Creating Supportive Environments:

- Schools and Universities: Implement comprehensive mental health programs in educational institutions. Provide counseling services, stress management workshops, and peer support groups.

- Workplaces: Foster a supportive work environment that prioritizes employee well-being. Offer mental health resources, flexible work arrangements, and create a culture of openness and support.

4. Encouraging Healthy Digital Habits:

- Digital Literacy: Educate Gen Z on healthy digital habits and the impact of screen time on mental health.

Promote digital detoxes and encourage balanced use of technology.

- Safe Social Media Use: Encourage safe and positive social media use. Advocate for platforms to implement stronger measures against cyberbullying and harmful content.

5. Strengthening Social Connections:

- Community Engagement: Encourage Gen Z to participate in community activities and volunteer work. Building strong community connections can combat social isolation and provide a sense of belonging.

- Family Support: Strengthen family support systems by encouraging open communication about mental health. Families play a crucial role in providing emotional support and recognizing signs of mental health issues.

Opportunities for Innovation and Improvement

There are numerous opportunities to innovate and improve mental health support for Gen Z, leveraging technology, research, and collaborative efforts.

1. Innovative Mental Health Technologies:

- Mental Health Apps: Develop and promote mental health apps that offer resources, self-help tools, and connections to professional support. Apps can provide accessible, on-the-go mental health support.

- AI and Machine Learning: Utilize AI and machine learning to create personalized mental health interventions.

Predictive analytics can help identify at-risk individuals and tailor support to their specific needs.

2. Research and Data Collection:

- Mental Health Studies: Conduct comprehensive studies on the mental health of Gen Z to better understand the specific challenges they face. Research can inform targeted interventions and policy decisions.

- Data-Driven Solutions: Use data to track the effectiveness of mental health programs and services. Continuous evaluation and improvement based on data can enhance the impact of mental health initiatives.

3. Policy and Advocacy:

- Mental Health Legislation: Advocate for policies that prioritize mental health funding, access to care, and support for mental health programs in schools and workplaces.

- Youth Involvement: Involve Gen Z in mental health advocacy and policy-making. Their perspectives and experiences are crucial for developing effective and relevant mental health initiatives.

Case Studies of Effective Mental Health Programs

Examining successful mental health programs provides insights into effective strategies for supporting Gen Z.

1. The Jed Foundation (JED):

- Comprehensive Support: JED works to protect emotional health and prevent suicide among teens and young adults. They partner with high schools and colleges to strengthen their mental health, substance misuse, and suicide prevention programs.

- Impact: JED's programs have been shown to increase help-seeking behavior and improve mental health outcomes among students. Their comprehensive approach includes education, policy advocacy, and community engagement.

2. Headspace:

- Mindfulness and Meditation: Headspace is a popular app that offers guided meditation and mindfulness exercises. It provides resources for managing stress, improving focus, and enhancing overall well-being.

- Impact: The app's user-friendly design and evidence-based practices have made it a valuable tool for Gen Z seeking to improve their mental health. Headspace's accessibility and affordability make it an effective resource.

3. University Mental Health Programs:

- Case Study: University of Michigan: The University of Michigan offers a comprehensive mental health program that includes counseling services, wellness workshops, peer support groups, and crisis intervention.

- Impact: The university's holistic approach addresses the diverse needs of its student population, promoting a culture of mental well-being and support.

Generation Z faces unique mental health challenges influenced by digital connectivity, economic uncertainty, academic pressures, and global events. Addressing these challenges requires a multifaceted approach that includes raising awareness, enhancing access to services, creating supportive environments, and promoting healthy digital habits. Opportunities for innovation and improvement abound, from leveraging technology and data to advocating for policy changes and involving Gen Z in the development of mental health initiatives. By understanding and addressing the specific mental health needs of Gen Z, society can support this generation in navigating their challenges and fostering their well-being.

The Digital Divide and Access to Technology

Generation Z, born approximately between 1997 and 2012, is often considered the first truly digital native generation. However, access to technology is not uniform across different regions and socioeconomic backgrounds, creating a digital divide that impacts education, career opportunities, and social inclusion. This chapter explores the digital divide affecting Gen Z, the factors contributing to this divide, and strategies for bridging the gap to ensure equitable access to technology.

Understanding the Digital Divide

The digital divide refers to the gap between those who have easy access to modern information and communication technology (ICT) and those who do not. This divide can manifest in various forms:

1. Access to Devices:

- Availability: Not all Gen Z individuals have access to personal devices such as laptops, tablets, or smartphones. Limited access to these devices can hinder their ability to participate fully in digital activities.

- Quality: The quality of devices can vary significantly. Older, less powerful devices may not support the latest applications or provide a satisfactory user experience, affecting productivity and learning.

2. Internet Connectivity:

- Broadband Access: High-speed internet access is essential for engaging with digital content, but it is not universally available. Rural areas and economically disadvantaged communities often lack reliable broadband access.

- Data Affordability: Even in areas with internet access, the cost of data can be prohibitive for some families.

This limits the amount of time Gen Z can spend online and restricts their ability to access educational and recreational resources.

3. Digital Literacy:

- Skills and Training: Digital literacy involves not only access to technology but also the skills to use it effectively. There is a significant gap in digital literacy skills, often influenced by the quality of education and available training resources.

- Parental Support: In households where parents or guardians have low digital literacy, young people may receive less support and guidance in navigating digital environments, further widening the divide.

Factors Contributing to the Digital Divide

Several factors contribute to the digital divide, exacerbating inequalities and limiting opportunities for those affected.

1. Socioeconomic Status:

- Income Disparities: Families with lower incomes are less likely to afford the latest technology and high-speed internet. This economic barrier directly impacts the digital experiences of Gen Z individuals from disadvantaged backgrounds.

- Educational Inequality: Schools in low-income areas often have fewer resources, including outdated technology and limited access to digital tools. This disparity in educational resources contributes to the digital divide.

2. Geographical Disparities:

- Urban vs. Rural: Urban areas typically have better infrastructure and more readily available high-speed internet compared to rural areas. Gen Z individuals in rural locations often face significant challenges in accessing digital resources.

- Global Differences: The digital divide is more pronounced in developing countries, where infrastructure development lags behind. Limited access to technology and the internet restricts the opportunities available to Gen Z in these regions.

3. Cultural and Social Barriers:

- Language and Content: The availability of digital content in different languages and culturally relevant materials can affect accessibility. Gen Z individuals who do not speak dominant languages may find it harder to engage with online content.

- Gender Inequality: In some cultures, gender norms and expectations can limit access to technology for young women. Addressing these social barriers is essential for closing the digital divide.

Impact of the Digital Divide on Gen Z

The digital divide has far-reaching consequences for Gen Z, affecting various aspects of their lives.

1. Educational Opportunities:

- Remote Learning: The COVID-19 pandemic highlighted the importance of digital access for education. Students without reliable internet and devices struggled to participate in remote learning, exacerbating educational inequalities.

- Skill Development: Limited access to technology hinders the development of digital skills, which are increasingly important for academic success and future employment.

2. Career Prospects:

- Job Market Readiness: Many jobs require digital proficiency, and those without access to technology and training are at a disadvantage in the job market. This can lead to lower employment rates and income disparities.

- Entrepreneurial Opportunities: Access to digital tools is crucial for entrepreneurial ventures. The digital divide restricts opportunities for Gen Z entrepreneurs to innovate and reach wider markets.

3. Social Inclusion:

- Connection and Community: Technology plays a vital role in social interactions and community building. The digital divide can lead to social isolation and exclusion, particularly for marginalized groups.

- Access to Information: The internet is a key source of information on health, social issues, and civic engagement. Limited access can leave Gen Z individuals less informed and less able to participate fully in society.

Strategies for Bridging the Digital Divide

Addressing the digital divide requires a coordinated effort from governments, educational institutions, businesses, and communities. Here are several strategies to bridge the gap:

1. Improving Infrastructure and Access:

- Broadband Expansion: Governments and private sector partnerships should invest in expanding broadband infrastructure, particularly in rural and underserved areas. Providing affordable high-speed internet is crucial for bridging the divide.

- Subsidized Devices: Programs that provide subsidized or free devices to low-income families can help ensure that all Gen Z individuals have access to the necessary tools for digital engagement.

2. Enhancing Digital Literacy:

- Educational Programs: Schools should incorporate digital literacy into their curricula, teaching students how to use technology effectively and safely. Community centers and libraries can also offer digital literacy programs for all ages.

- Parental Training: Providing digital literacy training for parents and guardians can empower them to support their children's digital learning and usage.

3. Promoting Inclusive Policies:

- Equitable Education Funding: Ensuring equitable funding for schools in low-income areas can help provide the resources needed for digital learning, including up-to-date technology and internet access.

- Addressing Social Barriers: Policies and programs that address gender inequality and other social barriers to technology access are essential. Promoting cultural and linguistic diversity in digital content can also enhance accessibility.

4. Leveraging Public-Private Partnerships:

- Corporate Initiatives: Businesses can play a role by offering technology grants, developing affordable devices, and investing in community programs that enhance digital access and literacy.

- Collaborative Efforts: Collaboration between governments, non-profits, and private companies can create comprehensive solutions to address the digital divide. These partnerships can leverage resources and expertise to maximize impact.

Case Studies of Successful Interventions

Examining successful initiatives provides insights into effective strategies for bridging the digital divide.

1. Google's Project Loon:

- Connecting Remote Areas: Project Loon uses high-altitude balloons to provide internet access to remote and underserved areas. This innovative approach has successfully brought connectivity to parts of Kenya and Peru.

- Impact: By providing internet access in remote areas, Project Loon has enabled students to participate in online learning, improved access to information, and facilitated economic opportunities.

2. One Laptop per Child (OLPC):

- Affordable Devices: OLPC aims to provide affordable, rugged laptops to children in developing countries. The program focuses on enhancing educational opportunities through technology.

- Impact: The initiative has improved digital literacy and educational outcomes in several countries, demonstrating the power of affordable technology in bridging the digital divide.

3. UK's National Centre for Computing Education (NCCE):

- Digital Literacy Education: The NCCE provides resources and training to schools across the UK to enhance computing education. Their programs aim to improve digital literacy and prepare students for the digital economy.

- Impact: By integrating computing education into the school curriculum, the NCCE has improved students' digital skills and readiness for future careers, helping to narrow the digital skills gap.

The digital divide presents significant challenges for Generation Z, affecting their educational opportunities, career prospects, and social inclusion. Addressing this divide requires a comprehensive approach that includes improving infrastructure, enhancing digital literacy, promoting inclusive policies, and leveraging public-private partnerships. Successful initiatives from around the world demonstrate that it is possible to bridge the gap and ensure that all Gen Z individuals have the opportunity to thrive in a digital world. By understanding and addressing the factors contributing to the digital divide, society can create a more equitable and inclusive future for this digital-native generation.

Opportunities for Growth and Empowerment

Generation Z, born approximately between 1997 and 2012, is poised to be one of the most dynamic and influential generations in history. While they face unique challenges, they also have unprecedented opportunities for growth and empowerment. This chapter explores these opportunities, examining how Gen Z can leverage their strengths, skills, and values to drive positive change in various areas, including education, career, entrepreneurship, social activism, and personal development.

Education and Lifelong Learning

Gen Z has access to an abundance of educational resources and opportunities that can empower them to achieve their full potential.

1. Online Learning Platforms:

- Accessible Education: Platforms like Coursera, edX, and Khan Academy provide access to high-quality education from top institutions worldwide. Gen Z can learn new skills, earn certifications, and pursue interests at their own pace.

- Skill Diversification: Online learning allows Gen Z to diversify their skill sets beyond traditional academic subjects. They can explore coding, digital marketing, graphic design, and more, enhancing their employability and adaptability.

2. Blended Learning Models:

- Hybrid Education: The integration of online and in-person learning offers flexibility and personalized learning experiences. Blended learning models can cater to different learning styles and needs, making education more inclusive and effective.

- Innovative Pedagogies: Schools and universities are increasingly adopting innovative pedagogical approaches, such as flipped classrooms and project-based learning. These methods encourage critical thinking, creativity, and practical application of knowledge.

3. Global Collaboration:

- Cross-Cultural Exchange: Digital platforms facilitate global collaboration, allowing Gen Z to engage with peers from different cultures and backgrounds. This exposure enhances cultural awareness and fosters a global mindset.

- International Programs: Opportunities for international exchange programs, internships, and virtual collaborations can broaden Gen Z's horizons and prepare them for a globalized world.

Career Development and Entrepreneurship

Gen Z's career aspirations are characterized by a desire for meaningful work, flexibility, and innovation. They have numerous opportunities to shape their professional paths.

1. Remote Work and Gig Economy:

- Flexibility and Autonomy: The rise of remote work and the gig economy offers Gen Z flexibility and autonomy in their careers. They can choose projects that align with their interests and values, work from anywhere, and balance personal and professional commitments.

- Skill Utilization: The gig economy allows Gen Z to leverage their diverse skills and talents. They can take on freelance projects, consult, or start side hustles, gaining valuable experience and building their portfolios.

2. Entrepreneurial Ventures:

- Startups and Innovation: Gen Z's entrepreneurial spirit drives them to start their own businesses and innovate in various fields. Access to digital tools, crowdfunding platforms, and startup incubators supports their entrepreneurial endeavors.

- Social Entrepreneurship: Many Gen Z entrepreneurs focus on social impact, creating businesses that address societal challenges. Social entrepreneurship combines profit with purpose, aligning with Gen Z's value-driven approach to business.

3. Professional Development Programs:

- Mentorship and Coaching: Access to mentorship and coaching programs can significantly enhance Gen Z's career development. Experienced professionals can provide guidance, support, and valuable insights.

- Corporate Training: Companies offering comprehensive training and development programs can attract and retain Gen Z talent. Opportunities for continuous learning and career advancement are crucial for this generation.

Social Activism and Civic Engagement

Gen Z is highly engaged in social activism and civic participation, driven by a desire to create positive change.

1. Digital Activism:

- Social Media Campaigns: Gen Z effectively uses social media to raise awareness, mobilize support, and advocate for social justice issues. Platforms like Twitter, Instagram, and TikTok are powerful tools for digital activism.

- Online Petitions and Fundraising: Digital tools enable Gen Z to organize online petitions, crowdfunding campaigns, and virtual events. These initiatives can drive tangible change and support causes they care about.

2. Community Involvement:

- Local Initiatives: Many Gen Z individuals are involved in local community initiatives, volunteering their time and skills to address local issues. Community involvement fosters a sense of belonging and impact.

- Youth Councils and Advisory Boards: Participating in youth councils and advisory boards allows Gen Z to influence policy and decision-making at local, national, and international levels. Their perspectives are crucial for creating youth-friendly policies.

3. Sustainable Practices:

- Environmental Advocacy: Gen Z is at the forefront of environmental advocacy, promoting sustainable practices and pushing for policies to combat climate change. Their activism includes organizing climate strikes, advocating for renewable energy, and supporting conservation efforts.

- Conscious Consumption: Gen Z's preference for sustainable and ethical products drives demand for responsible business practices. They support brands that prioritize sustainability, fair trade, and social responsibility.

Personal Development and Well-Being

Fostering personal development and well-being is essential for Gen Z's growth and empowerment.

1. Mental Health Awareness:

- Support Systems: Access to mental health resources and support systems is crucial for Gen Z. Schools, workplaces, and communities should prioritize mental well-being and provide necessary support.

- Mindfulness and Self-Care: Practices such as mindfulness, meditation, and self-care can help Gen Z manage stress and anxiety. Encouraging these practices promotes overall well-being and resilience.

2. Physical Health and Fitness:

- Active Lifestyles: Promoting active lifestyles through sports, fitness programs, and recreational activities supports physical health. Access to gyms, parks, and wellness centers is essential for maintaining an active lifestyle.

- Healthy Eating: Nutrition education and access to healthy food options are vital for Gen Z's physical health. Schools and communities should promote balanced diets and healthy eating habits.

3. Financial Literacy:

- Budgeting and Saving: Financial literacy programs can equip Gen Z with the skills to manage their finances effectively. Understanding budgeting, saving, and investing is crucial for financial stability and independence.

- Entrepreneurial Finance: For aspiring entrepreneurs, knowledge of business finance, fundraising, and investment is essential. Educational resources and mentorship can support their entrepreneurial ventures.

Case Studies of Empowerment Initiatives

Examining successful initiatives provides insights into effective strategies for empowering Gen Z.

1. Khan Academy:

- Accessible Education: Khan Academy offers free online courses and educational resources, making high-quality education accessible to all. The platform's interactive content supports self-paced learning and skill development.

- Impact: Khan Academy's global reach has empowered millions of students to pursue their educational goals, bridging gaps in access to education.

2. Youth Climate Strikes:

- Environmental Advocacy: Inspired by Greta Thunberg, youth climate strikes have mobilized Gen Z around the world to demand action on climate change. These strikes highlight the urgency of environmental issues and the power of youth activism.

- Impact: The movement has influenced public discourse and policy, raising awareness about climate change and pushing for legislative action.

3. LinkedIn Learning:

- Professional Development: LinkedIn Learning provides online courses and training programs for professional development. Gen Z can access a wide range of topics, from technical skills to leadership and personal growth.

- Impact: The platform supports continuous learning and career advancement, helping Gen Z stay competitive in the job market.

Generation Z is uniquely positioned to leverage the opportunities available to them for growth and empowerment. Through accessible education, innovative career paths, social activism, and a focus on personal well-being, they can drive positive change and achieve their full potential. By supporting Gen Z in navigating these opportunities, society can benefit from their creativity, resilience, and commitment to making the world a better place. Understanding and fostering the strengths of Gen Z is essential for building a future that is inclusive, sustainable, and empowered.

Opportunities for Growth and Empowerment

Generation Z, born approximately between 1997 and 2012, is a generation uniquely positioned to leverage the rapidly evolving landscape of technology, social change, and global connectivity. While they face distinct challenges, they also have unprecedented opportunities for growth and empowerment. This chapter explores these opportunities, examining how Gen Z can harness their strengths, skills, and values to drive positive change in education, careers, entrepreneurship, social activism, and personal development.

Education and Lifelong Learning

Gen Z has access to an unparalleled range of educational resources and opportunities that can empower them to achieve their full potential.

1. Online Learning Platforms:

- Accessible Education: Platforms like Coursera, edX, and Khan Academy provide access to high-quality education from top institutions worldwide. Gen Z can learn new skills, earn certifications, and pursue interests at their own pace.

- Skill Diversification: Online learning allows Gen Z to diversify their skill sets beyond traditional academic subjects. They can explore coding, digital marketing, graphic design, and more, enhancing their employability and adaptability.

2. Blended Learning Models:

- Hybrid Education: The integration of online and in-person learning offers flexibility and personalized learning experiences. Blended learning models can cater to different learning styles and needs, making education more inclusive and effective.

- Innovative Pedagogies: Schools and universities are increasingly adopting innovative pedagogical approaches, such as flipped classrooms and project-based learning. These methods encourage critical thinking, creativity, and practical application of knowledge.

3. Global Collaboration:

- Cross-Cultural Exchange: Digital platforms facilitate global collaboration, allowing Gen Z to engage with peers from different cultures and backgrounds. This exposure enhances cultural awareness and fosters a global mindset.

- International Programs: Opportunities for international exchange programs, internships, and virtual collaborations can broaden Gen Z's horizons and prepare them for a globalized world.

Career Development and Entrepreneurship

Gen Z's career aspirations are characterized by a desire for meaningful work, flexibility, and innovation. They have numerous opportunities to shape their professional paths.

1. Remote Work and the Gig Economy:

- Flexibility and Autonomy: The rise of remote work and the gig economy offers Gen Z flexibility and autonomy in their careers. They can choose projects that align with their interests and values, work from anywhere, and balance personal and professional commitments.

- Skill Utilization: The gig economy allows Gen Z to leverage their diverse skills and talents. They can take on freelance projects, consult, or start side hustles, gaining valuable experience and building their portfolios.

2. Entrepreneurial Ventures:

- Startups and Innovation: Gen Z's entrepreneurial spirit drives them to start their own businesses and innovate in various fields. Access to digital tools, crowdfunding platforms, and startup incubators supports their entrepreneurial endeavors.

- Social Entrepreneurship: Many Gen Z entrepreneurs focus on social impact, creating businesses that address societal challenges. Social entrepreneurship combines profit with purpose, aligning with Gen Z's value-driven approach to business.

3. Professional Development Programs:

- Mentorship and Coaching: Access to mentorship and coaching programs can significantly enhance Gen Z's career development. Experienced professionals can provide guidance, support, and valuable insights.

- Corporate Training: Companies offering comprehensive training and development programs can attract and retain Gen Z talent. Opportunities for continuous learning and career advancement are crucial for this generation.

Social Activism and Civic Engagement

Gen Z is highly engaged in social activism and civic participation, driven by a desire to create positive change.

1. Digital Activism:

- Social Media Campaigns: Gen Z effectively uses social media to raise awareness, mobilize support, and advocate for social justice issues. Platforms like Twitter, Instagram, and TikTok are powerful tools for digital activism.

- Online Petitions and Fundraising: Digital tools enable Gen Z to organize online petitions, crowdfunding campaigns, and virtual events. These initiatives can drive tangible change and support causes they care about.

2. Community Involvement:

- Local Initiatives: Many Gen Z individuals are involved in local community initiatives, volunteering their time and skills to address local issues. Community involvement fosters a sense of belonging and impact.

- Youth Councils and Advisory Boards: Participating in youth councils and advisory boards allows Gen Z to influence policy and decision-making at local, national, and international levels. Their perspectives are crucial for creating youth-friendly policies.

3. Sustainable Practices:

- Environmental Advocacy: Gen Z is at the forefront of environmental advocacy, promoting sustainable practices and pushing for policies to combat climate change. Their activism includes organizing climate strikes, advocating for renewable energy, and supporting conservation efforts.

- Conscious Consumption: Gen Z's preference for sustainable and ethical products drives demand for responsible business practices. They support brands that prioritize sustainability, fair trade, and social responsibility.

Personal Development and Well-Being

Fostering personal development and well-being is essential for Gen Z's growth and empowerment.

1. Mental Health Awareness:

- Support Systems: Access to mental health resources and support systems is crucial for Gen Z. Schools, workplaces, and communities should prioritize mental well-being and provide necessary support.

- Mindfulness and Self-Care: Practices such as mindfulness, meditation, and self-care can help Gen Z manage stress and anxiety. Encouraging these practices promotes overall well-being and resilience.

2. Physical Health and Fitness:

- Active Lifestyles: Promoting active lifestyles through sports, fitness programs, and recreational activities supports physical health. Access to gyms, parks, and wellness centers is essential for maintaining an active lifestyle.

- Healthy Eating: Nutrition education and access to healthy food options are vital for Gen Z's physical health. Schools and communities should promote balanced diets and healthy eating habits.

3. Financial Literacy:

- Budgeting and Saving: Financial literacy programs can equip Gen Z with the skills to manage their finances effectively. Understanding budgeting, saving, and investing is crucial for financial stability and independence.

- Entrepreneurial Finance: For aspiring entrepreneurs, knowledge of business finance, fundraising, and investment is essential. Educational resources and mentorship can support their entrepreneurial ventures.

Case Studies of Empowerment Initiatives

Examining successful initiatives provides insights into effective strategies for empowering Gen Z.

1. Khan Academy:

- Accessible Education: Khan Academy offers free online courses and educational resources, making high-quality education accessible to all. The platform's interactive content supports self-paced learning and skill development.

- Impact: Khan Academy's global reach has empowered millions of students to pursue their educational goals, bridging gaps in access to education.

2. Youth Climate Strikes:

- Environmental Advocacy: Inspired by Greta Thunberg, youth climate strikes have mobilized Gen Z around the world to demand action on climate change. These strikes highlight the urgency of environmental issues and the power of youth activism.

- Impact: The movement has influenced public discourse and policy, raising awareness about climate change and pushing for legislative action.

3. LinkedIn Learning:

- Professional Development: LinkedIn Learning provides online courses and training programs for professional development. Gen Z can access a wide range of topics, from technical skills to leadership and personal growth.

- Impact: The platform supports continuous learning and career advancement, helping Gen Z stay competitive in the job market.

Generation Z is uniquely positioned to leverage the opportunities available to them for growth and empowerment. Through accessible education, innovative career paths, social activism, and a focus on personal well-being, they can drive positive change and achieve their full potential. By supporting Gen Z in navigating these opportunities, society can benefit from their creativity, resilience, and commitment to making the world a better place. Understanding and fostering the strengths of Gen Z is essential for building a future that is inclusive, sustainable, and empowered.

CHAPTER 12

CONCLUSION

Summary of Key Findings

Generation Z, born approximately between 1997 and 2012, represents a dynamic and influential demographic with unique characteristics, challenges, and opportunities. Over the course of this book, we have explored various aspects of Gen Z's lives, including their values, behaviors, mental health, digital habits, career aspirations, and social activism. This chapter provides a summary of the key findings from each chapter, highlighting the critical insights that define Gen Z and their impact on the world.

Key Characteristics and Values

1. Digital Natives:

- Gen Z is the first generation to grow up with the internet, social media, and smartphones. Their digital fluency shapes their communication, learning, and entertainment preferences.

- They are comfortable navigating multiple digital platforms, integrating technology seamlessly into their daily lives.

2. Value-Driven and Socially Conscious:

- Gen Z places a high value on authenticity, transparency, and ethical behavior. They support brands and organizations that align with their values.

- They are deeply concerned about social justice, environmental sustainability, and inclusivity, actively participating in advocacy and activism.

3. Mental Health Awareness:

- Mental health is a significant concern for Gen Z, with high levels of stress, anxiety, and depression reported among this cohort.

- They are more open to discussing mental health issues and seeking help, advocating for greater awareness and support.

Educational Aspirations and Learning Preferences

4. Lifelong Learning:

- Gen Z embraces lifelong learning, utilizing online platforms and resources to continuously acquire new skills and knowledge.

- They prefer flexible, personalized learning experiences that cater to their individual needs and interests.

5. Blended Learning Models:

- The integration of online and in-person learning provides Gen Z with the flexibility and adaptability they seek in education.

- Innovative pedagogical approaches, such as flipped classrooms and project-based learning, enhance their engagement and critical thinking skills.

Career Development and Entrepreneurship

6. Remote Work and Gig Economy:

- The rise of remote work and the gig economy aligns with Gen Z's desire for flexibility and autonomy in their careers.

- They leverage their diverse skills and talents in freelance projects and entrepreneurial ventures, often focusing on social impact.

7. Entrepreneurial Spirit:

- Many Gen Z individuals are driven to start their own businesses and innovate in various fields. They utilize digital tools and platforms to support their entrepreneurial endeavors.

- Social entrepreneurship is prevalent, with a focus on creating businesses that address societal challenges and contribute to positive change.

Social Activism and Civic Engagement

8. Digital Activism:

- Gen Z effectively uses social media to raise awareness, mobilize support, and advocate for social justice issues. Platforms like Twitter, Instagram, and TikTok are powerful tools for their activism.

- Online petitions, crowdfunding campaigns, and virtual events are common methods for driving tangible change.

9. Community Involvement:

- Many Gen Z individuals actively participate in local community initiatives, volunteering their time and skills to address local issues.

- Involvement in youth councils and advisory boards allows them to influence policy and decision-making at various levels.

Personal Development and Well-Being

10. Mental and Physical Health:

- Access to mental health resources and support systems is crucial for Gen Z's well-being. They prioritize practices such as mindfulness, meditation, and self-care to manage stress and anxiety.

- Promoting active lifestyles and healthy eating habits supports their physical health, with an emphasis on balanced diets and fitness programs.

11. Financial Literacy:

- Financial literacy programs equip Gen Z with the skills to manage their finances effectively. Understanding budgeting, saving, and investing is essential for their financial stability and independence.

- Knowledge of business finance, fundraising, and investment supports their entrepreneurial ventures.

Addressing the Digital Divide

12. Bridging the Gap:

- The digital divide presents significant challenges for Gen Z, affecting their educational opportunities, career prospects, and social inclusion.

- Addressing this divide requires improving infrastructure, enhancing digital literacy, promoting inclusive policies, and leveraging public-private partnerships.

Case Studies and Success Stories

13. Empowerment Initiatives:

- Successful initiatives like Khan Academy, youth climate strikes, and LinkedIn Learning provide insights into effective strategies for empowering Gen Z.

- These programs highlight the importance of accessible education, professional development, and environmental advocacy in supporting Gen Z's growth and empowerment.

Generation Z is uniquely positioned to leverage the opportunities available to them for growth and empowerment. Their digital fluency, value-driven mindset, entrepreneurial spirit, and commitment to social justice and sustainability make them a powerful force for positive change. By understanding and fostering the strengths of Gen Z, society can build a future that is inclusive, sustainable, and empowered. Supporting Gen Z in navigating their challenges and maximizing their opportunities is essential for creating a better world for all.

The Evolving Nature of Gen Z

Generation Z, born approximately between 1997 and 2012, is a generation characterized by their adaptability, digital fluency, and strong value-driven mindset. As they continue to mature, their influence on society, culture, and the global economy is becoming increasingly apparent. This chapter explores the evolving nature of Gen Z, focusing on how they are shaping and being shaped by the world around them, and what the future holds for this dynamic generation.

Adaptability and Resilience

Gen Z has demonstrated remarkable adaptability and resilience in the face of rapid technological advancements and global upheavals.

1. Adaptation to Technological Change:

   - Early Adopters: Gen Z is quick to adopt new technologies, integrating them seamlessly into their personal and professional lives. Their comfort with technology positions them as leaders in driving digital innovation.

   - Continuous Learning: Their commitment to lifelong learning and skill diversification allows them to stay ahead in a rapidly changing job market. They are adept at using online platforms to acquire new knowledge and skills.

2. Resilience Amidst Global Challenges:

   - Pandemic Response: The COVID-19 pandemic tested Gen Z's resilience, forcing them to adapt to remote learning, work, and socializing. Their ability to navigate these changes has strengthened their capacity to cope with future uncertainties.

   - Climate Activism: Faced with the existential threat of climate change, Gen Z has shown resilience and determination in advocating for environmental sustainability. Their activism has brought global attention to the urgent need for climate action.

Digital Fluency and Innovation

Gen Z's digital fluency is a defining characteristic that continues to evolve, influencing various aspects of their lives and society.

1. Innovation in Digital Spaces:

- Content Creation: Gen Z is at the forefront of content creation on platforms like TikTok, YouTube, and Instagram. They are redefining media consumption and production, often turning their digital presence into entrepreneurial ventures.

- Digital Entrepreneurship: Leveraging digital tools and platforms, Gen Z entrepreneurs are creating innovative business models and disrupting traditional industries. Their ventures often focus on technology, sustainability, and social impact.

2. Revolutionizing Communication:

- Social Media: Gen Z's use of social media goes beyond entertainment; it is a powerful tool for communication, activism, and community building. They are setting trends and influencing public discourse on these platforms.

- Virtual Reality and AI: As virtual reality (VR) and artificial intelligence (AI) technologies advance, Gen Z is exploring their potential in various fields, from gaming and entertainment to education and healthcare.

Value-Driven Mindset

Gen Z's values play a crucial role in shaping their behaviors, choices, and impact on society.

1. Commitment to Social Justice:

- Advocacy and Activism: Gen Z is deeply committed to social justice issues, including racial equality, gender rights, and LGBTQ+ rights. Their activism is both online and offline, influencing policy changes and societal attitudes.

- Corporate Accountability: They hold businesses accountable for their social and environmental impact, demanding transparency and ethical practices. Brands that fail to align with these values risk losing Gen Z's support.

2. Focus on Sustainability:

- Environmental Consciousness: Gen Z prioritizes sustainability in their consumption habits, supporting eco-friendly products and companies that practice environmental stewardship. Their influence is driving the green economy.

- Sustainable Innovation: In their entrepreneurial and professional endeavors, Gen Z seeks to innovate sustainably. They are developing solutions that address environmental challenges while promoting economic growth.

Future Prospects and Influence

As Gen Z continues to grow and assert their influence, their impact on the future will be profound and multifaceted.

1. Shaping the Workforce:

- Redefining Work Norms: Gen Z's preference for flexibility, remote work, and work-life balance is reshaping traditional work norms. Employers must adapt to these preferences to attract and retain top talent.

- Skill-Based Economy: Their focus on continuous learning and skill development supports the transition to a skill-based economy. Gen Z values practical skills and experiential learning over traditional credentials.

2. Driving Economic and Social Change:

- Economic Impact: As consumers, entrepreneurs, and professionals, Gen Z's economic influence will continue to grow. Their spending habits and investment choices are already impacting markets and industries.

- Social Transformation: Gen Z's commitment to social justice, inclusivity, and sustainability will drive significant social transformations. Their activism and advocacy will shape policies and societal norms for years to come.

3. Global Connectivity:

- Cross-Cultural Engagement: Gen Z's global connectivity fosters cross-cultural understanding and collaboration. Their ability to engage with peers worldwide positions them as global citizens who can address international challenges.

- Digital Diplomacy: As digital natives, Gen Z is well-equipped to engage in digital diplomacy, using technology to build bridges across cultural and national divides. Their global perspective will be crucial in navigating future geopolitical landscapes.

Generation Z is a generation of adaptability, resilience, digital fluency, and strong values. Their evolving nature is characterized by their ability to navigate and influence a rapidly changing world. As they continue to grow, their impact on technology, the economy, social justice, and global connectivity will be profound. Understanding and supporting Gen Z's journey is essential for fostering a future that is inclusive, sustainable, and empowered. The evolving nature of Gen Z presents both challenges and opportunities, and their unique perspectives and skills are invaluable assets in shaping a better world for all.

Preparing for the Future: Insights for Parents, Educators, and Marketers

As Generation Z, born approximately between 1997 and 2012, continues to grow and shape the future, it is crucial for parents, educators, and marketers to understand their unique characteristics and needs. This chapter provides insights and strategies for effectively supporting and engaging Gen Z in their personal development, education, and consumer behavior.

Insights for Parents

Parents play a vital role in nurturing the development and well-being of Gen Z. Understanding their children's needs and adapting parenting strategies accordingly can significantly impact their growth.

1. Support Mental Health and Well-Being:

- Open Communication: Encourage open and honest communication about mental health. Create a safe space for Gen Z to express their feelings and concerns without judgment.

- Access to Resources: Ensure access to mental health resources, such as counseling, support groups, and mindfulness practices. Teach coping mechanisms for managing stress and anxiety.

2. Foster Digital Literacy and Healthy Habits:

- Digital Education: Educate Gen Z about responsible and safe internet use. Discuss the importance of digital literacy, privacy, and cybersecurity.

- Balanced Screen Time: Promote a healthy balance between screen time and offline activities. Encourage physical activities, hobbies, and family interactions to reduce excessive screen use.

3. Encourage Lifelong Learning:

- Support Diverse Interests: Recognize and support Gen Z's diverse interests and passions. Provide opportunities for them to explore different fields and activities.

- Promote Critical Thinking: Encourage critical thinking and problem-solving skills. Discuss current events, ethical dilemmas, and encourage independent research.

4. Model Value-Driven Behavior:

- Lead by Example: Model behaviors that reflect values of sustainability, inclusivity, and social responsibility. Involve Gen Z in family decisions that align with these values.

- Community Involvement: Engage in community service and activism as a family. Demonstrating a commitment to social causes can inspire similar values in Gen Z.

Insights for Educators

Educators have a significant influence on shaping Gen Z's educational experiences and preparing them for future challenges. Adapting teaching methods to meet their needs can enhance learning outcomes.

1. Integrate Technology in Education:

- Blended Learning: Incorporate a mix of online and in-person learning to provide flexibility and cater to different learning styles. Use digital tools to enhance engagement and interactivity.

- Digital Literacy Curriculum: Implement comprehensive digital literacy programs that teach students how to navigate the digital world safely and effectively.

2. Promote Collaborative and Experiential Learning:

- Project-Based Learning: Use project-based learning to encourage collaboration, creativity, and real-world problem-solving. Allow students to work on projects that interest them and address real-life challenges.

- Cross-Cultural Collaboration: Facilitate opportunities for cross-cultural collaboration through international projects, exchange programs, and virtual classrooms.

3. Support Mental and Emotional Well-Being:

- Mental Health Resources: Provide access to mental health resources within schools, such as counseling services, wellness programs, and peer support groups.

- Social-Emotional Learning (SEL): Incorporate SEL into the curriculum to help students develop emotional intelligence, resilience, and interpersonal skills.

4. Encourage Lifelong Learning and Critical Thinking:

- Curiosity and Inquiry: Foster a culture of curiosity and inquiry in the classroom. Encourage students to ask questions, explore new ideas, and pursue independent research.

- Ethical and Global Education: Teach students about global issues, ethics, and the impact of their actions on society and the environment. Encourage critical thinking about social and environmental justice.

Insights for Marketers

Marketers must understand Gen Z's preferences, values, and behaviors to effectively engage with them as consumers. Strategies that resonate with their digital fluency and value-driven mindset can build brand loyalty and trust.

1. Authenticity and Transparency:

- Genuine Messaging: Use authentic and transparent messaging that reflects the brand's values and mission. Avoid overly polished or insincere advertisements.

- Storytelling: Tell compelling stories that highlight real experiences, customer testimonials, and the brand's impact on society and the environment.

2. Leverage Digital Platforms and Influencers:

- Social Media Engagement: Engage with Gen Z on their preferred social media platforms. Create interactive and engaging content, such as challenges, polls, and live streams.

- Influencer Partnerships: Collaborate with influencers who align with the brand's values and resonate with Gen Z. Authentic endorsements from trusted influencers can enhance credibility and reach.

3. Promote Sustainability and Social Responsibility:

- Sustainable Practices: Highlight the brand's commitment to sustainability and ethical practices. Use eco-friendly packaging, support fair trade, and reduce the brand's environmental footprint.

- Social Impact Initiatives: Showcase the brand's involvement in social impact initiatives, such as charitable partnerships, community projects, and social justice campaigns.

4. Personalization and Interactive Experiences:

- Personalized Marketing: Use data-driven insights to personalize marketing efforts. Tailor recommendations, offers, and content to individual preferences and behaviors.

- Interactive Content: Create interactive and immersive experiences, such as augmented reality (AR) and virtual reality (VR) campaigns, to engage Gen Z in meaningful ways.

Case Studies of Effective Engagement

Examining successful engagement strategies provides valuable insights into how parents, educators, and marketers can effectively support and connect with Gen Z.

1. Nike's Social Media Campaigns:

- Digital Engagement: Nike's campaigns on platforms like Instagram and TikTok use interactive content, such as challenges and user-generated content, to engage Gen Z. Their storytelling emphasizes authenticity and social impact.

- Impact: Nike's focus on inclusivity, diversity, and sustainability resonates with Gen Z, building brand loyalty and fostering a strong emotional connection with their audience.

2. Harvard University's Online Learning Initiatives:

- Accessible Education: Harvard offers a range of free and low-cost online courses through platforms like edX, providing access to high-quality education for learners worldwide.

- Impact: These initiatives support lifelong learning and skill development, empowering Gen Z to pursue their educational goals and adapt to a changing job market.

3. Headspace's Mental Health Resources:

- Supportive Environment: Headspace offers mindfulness and meditation resources to support mental health and well-being. Their app provides accessible tools for managing stress and anxiety.

- Impact: By promoting mental health awareness and providing practical resources, Headspace effectively addresses the needs of Gen Z and encourages healthy habits.

Preparing for the future with Generation Z requires a deep understanding of their unique characteristics, needs, and values. Parents, educators, and marketers each have a crucial role to play in supporting Gen Z's growth, development, and engagement. By fostering mental and emotional well-being, promoting lifelong learning, leveraging digital platforms, and emphasizing authenticity and social responsibility, we can empower Gen Z to navigate their challenges and seize their opportunities. Understanding and embracing the evolving nature of Gen Z is essential for building a future that is inclusive, sustainable, and empowered.

Surveys and Studies on Gen Z Behavior

1. Pew Research Center: "On the Cusp of Adulthood and Facing an Uncertain Future: What We Know About Gen Z So Far":

- This comprehensive study explores the demographic characteristics, values, and behaviors of Gen Z, focusing on their use of technology, social media habits, and political engagement.

2. McKinsey & Company: "True Gen: Generation Z and its Implications for Companies":

- This report examines the attitudes and behaviors of Gen Z, highlighting their digital fluency, value-driven mindset, and impact on consumer trends.

3. Deloitte: "Understanding Generation Z in the Workplace":

- Deloitte's study focuses on Gen Z's expectations and preferences in the workplace, including their desire for flexibility, career development, and work-life balance.

4. IBM Institute for Business Value: "Uniquely Generation Z":

- This research explores Gen Z's consumer behavior, emphasizing their demand for personalized experiences, brand authenticity, and social responsibility.

5. Center for Generational Kinetics: "The State of Gen Z 2020":

- This annual report provides insights into Gen Z's attitudes towards education, employment, technology, and social issues, based on extensive surveys and data analysis.

Glossary of Key Terms

1. Blended Learning: An educational approach that combines online digital media with traditional face-to-face classroom methods, allowing for flexible and personalized learning experiences.

2. Digital Literacy: The ability to effectively and critically navigate, evaluate, and create information using a range of digital technologies.

3. Gig Economy: A labor market characterized by the prevalence of short-term contracts or freelance work as opposed to permanent jobs.

4. Lifelong Learning: The ongoing, voluntary, and self-motivated pursuit of knowledge for personal or professional development throughout an individual's life.

5. Mental Health Awareness: Efforts to educate and inform the public about mental health issues, reduce stigma, and promote access to mental health resources and support.

6. Remote Work: A work arrangement in which employees do not commute to a central place of work but instead perform their job duties from a location of their choice, often using digital technology to stay connected.

7. Social Entrepreneurship: A business model that aims to address social, cultural, or environmental issues through innovative solutions, combining profit with purpose.

8. Sustainable Practices: Actions and strategies that seek to reduce negative impacts on the environment and promote long-term ecological balance.

9. Value-Driven Mindset: A perspective that prioritizes ethical behavior, social responsibility, and alignment with personal values in decision-making processes.

Additional Resources and Readings

1. Books:
    - "iGen: Why Today's Super-Connected Kids Are Growing Up Less Rebellious, More Tolerant, Less Happy— and Completely Unprepared for Adulthood" by Jean M. Twenge
    - "The Gen Z Effect: The Six Forces Shaping the Future of Business" by Thomas Koulopoulos and Dan Keldsen
    - "Generation Z Unfiltered: Facing Nine Hidden Challenges of the Most Anxious Population" by Tim Elmore and Andrew McPeak

2. Articles:
    - "How Generation Z Is Shaping the Change in Education" (Forbes)

- "The Unfiltered Truth About Generation Z" (Harvard Business Review)

- "Gen Z and the Future of Work: What Employers Need to Know" (SHRM)

3. Websites:

- Pew Research Center: www.pewresearch.org

- McKinsey & Company: www.mckinsey.com

- Deloitte Insights: www.deloitte.com/insights

4. Organizations:

- The Center for Generational Kinetics: www.genhq.com

- IBM Institute for Business Value: www.ibm.com/services/us/gbs/thoughtleadership

These appendices provide a wealth of information and resources for further understanding Generation Z's behavior, preferences, and impact. Whether you are a parent, educator, or marketer, these tools will help you better support and engage with this dynamic and influential generation.

REFERENCES

Academic Papers

1. Twenge, J. M. (2017). iGen: Why Today's Super-Connected Kids Are Growing Up Less Rebellious, More Tolerant, Less Happy—and Completely Unprepared for Adulthood. Atria Books.

2. Seemiller, C., & Grace, M. (2016). Generation Z Goes to College. Jossey-Bass.

3. Turner, A. (2015). Generation Z: Technology and Social Interest. The Journal of Individual Psychology, 71(2), 103-113.

Reports and Studies

4. Pew Research Center. (2020). On the Cusp of Adulthood and Facing an Uncertain Future: What We Know

About Gen Z So Far. Retrieved from https://www.pewresearch.org

5. McKinsey & Company. (2018). True Gen: Generation Z and its Implications for Companies. Retrieved from https://www.mckinsey.com

6. Deloitte. (2019). Understanding Generation Z in the Workplace. Retrieved from https://www2.deloitte.com

7. IBM Institute for Business Value. (2017). Uniquely Generation Z. Retrieved from https://www.ibm.com/services/us/gbs/thoughtleadership

8. Center for Generational Kinetics. (2020). The State of Gen Z 2020. Retrieved from https://genhq.com

Books

9. Koulopoulos, T., & Keldsen, D. (2014). The Gen Z Effect: The Six Forces Shaping the Future of Business. Bibliomotion.

10. Elmore, T., & McPeak, A. (2019). Generation Z Unfiltered: Facing Nine Hidden Challenges of the Most Anxious Population. Poet Gardener Publishing.

Articles

11. "How Generation Z Is Shaping the Change in Education." Forbes. Retrieved from https://www.forbes.com

12. "The Unfiltered Truth About Generation Z." Harvard Business Review. Retrieved from https://hbr.org

13. "Gen Z and the Future of Work: What Employers Need to Know." SHRM. Retrieved from https://www.shrm.org

Websites

14. Pew Research Center. Retrieved from https://www.pewresearch.org

15. McKinsey & Company. Retrieved from https://www.mckinsey.com

16. Deloitte Insights. Retrieved from https://www2.deloitte.com

17. IBM Institute for Business Value. Retrieved from https://www.ibm.com/services/us/gbs/thoughtleadership

18. The Center for Generational Kinetics. Retrieved from https://genhq.com

Case Studies and Examples

19. "Nike's Social Media Campaigns." Retrieved from https://www.nike.com

20. "Harvard University's Online Learning Initiatives." Retrieved from https://www.harvard.edu

21. "Headspace's Mental Health Resources." Retrieved from https://www.headspace.com

These references provide a comprehensive list of the academic papers, articles, books, reports, and online resources cited throughout the text. They offer additional insights and detailed research on the behaviors, preferences, and impact of Generation Z.